ZERSTÖRER GRUPPE

A History of V./(Z)LG 1 - I./NJG 3
1939-1941

LUDWIG V. EIMANNSBERGER

Translated from the German by David Johnston

Schiffer Military History
Atglen, PA

Acknowledgements

I wish to thank the survivors of V/LG 1, I/NJG 3 and other units and the families of the fallen or those who have died since the war for the writings and photographs used in this book: Rudolf Altendorf, Willfried Arndt, Hans Bechthold, Eckart v. Bonin, Horst Brüggow, Alois Dierkes, Karl Döpler, Karl Elchhorn, Hans Gaffal, Otto Giglhuber, Walter Grabmann, Herbert Grofle, Erich Heidrich, Joachim Jäckel, Rudolf Kobert, Hellmut Peters, Günther Radusch, Werner Schümichen, Alfred Stier, Rudolf Stöber, Peter Voelskow, Otto Weckeiser, Gustav Wiebe; *the families*: Banser, v. Boltenstern, Bruns, Busch, Clausen, Datz, Dieckmann, Fritz, Gröbl, Haarmann, Haas, Hessell, Jecke, Junge, Krebitz, Köpge (Becker), Lindemann, Müntefering, Meinhard, Petry, Reinhold, Schmergal, Schnoor, Seufert, Speier (Brill), Swietlik, Warrelmann. Weller, Würgatsch (Petschel), Zobel. In England help came from: the Commonwealth War Graves Commission, Royal Air Force Museum Hendon, Andy Saunders, John Vasco, Peter Cornwell, Alan Crouch, Victor Dutton, Chris Coss, Dennis Knight, Jack Walker, Peter Walker, Ron Watkins, Douglas Weller; in Germany WASt/Berlin, Gemeinschaft der Jagdflieger (Fighter Pilots Association, Horst Amberg), the German War Graves Commission, the Luftwaffe historian Hans Ring, Jochen Prien, Winfried Bock, Heinrich Weiss, members of JG 3, JG 27 (Leo Suschko, Eduard Neumann), the successor Gruppe I./NJG 3 (Paul Gärtig, Georg Habermann, Helmut Nagel, Willi Nicke, Konrad Rösner, Karl Schröder, Paul Zorner). This list is incomplete, therefore thank you to everyone who has helped.

Front dust jacket artwork by Steve Ferguson, Colorado Springs, CO.

LIENSBERGER'S LIMIT
Depicted is the harrowing tree top level pursuit of 149 Sqn. Hurricane pilot PO Burton only seconds from overtaking *Gruppenkommandeur* Liensberger on the fateful mission of September 27, 1940. See chapter six for further details.

Book Design by Robert Biondi.
Translated from the German by David Johnston.

Copyright © 1998 by Ludwig v. Eimannsberger.
Library of Congress Catalog Number: 97-80370.

Printed in the United States of America.
ISBN: 0-7643-0479-8

We are interested in hearing from authors with book ideas on related topics.

Published by Schiffer Publishing Ltd.
4880 Lower Valley Road
Atglen, PA 19310 USA
Phone: (610) 593-1777
FAX: (610) 593-2002
E-mail: Schifferbk@aol.com.
Please write for a free catalog.
This book may be purchased from the publisher.
Please include $3.95 postage.
Try your bookstore first.

CONTENTS

PREFACE

The writings presented here are the result of chance occurrence, a letter from England in 1986 concerning the Liensberger crash on September 27, 1940 (*Hptm.* Liensberger was the author's uncle). Surviving records led to further investigations. Contact was established with survivors and families of the fallen and those who died since the war. I wish to express my gratitude for their accounts, documents, photos, etc. All have their own painful memories of that time. Casualties, wounds – some with serious lasting effects – and captivity affected and tried many families. All of this left its mark on those men – whose average age at the time was just 23 years.

FOREWORD

by Hans-Hartmut Bechthold former pilot
14 Staffel, V/(Zerstörer) Lehrgeschwader 1

This book is a recollection of a difficult time. After many years we finally have a thorough, almost complete chronicle of our *"Zerstörergruppe."*

Training at Fürth, Schleissheim, Werneuchen and Stargard was followed by my transfer to V/(Z) LG 1 during the so-called *"Sitzkrieg."* There were missions over France and, from 4 July 1940, over England. During our operations over the Channel we flew a relatively large number of independent missions, although parallel or coordinated operations were carried out with II and III/ZG 76. The missions usually involved two or three *Staffeln*. We knew each other mainly from information at the mission briefings. The degree of familiarity between the pilots was probably very limited.

On 27 September 1940 I was shot down in my Bf 110, L1+GL, between London and the Channel on the way back from our mission. Unlike my radio operator Uffz. Koch, who was fatally hit in combat, I was fortunate to be able to bail out. I was taken prisoner by the British. For more than six years I and many others were prisoners of war in Canada. Through that whole long time we often discussed our last takeoffs and missions over France and England. My special memory – my first interrogation puzzled me and made me sad. They declared to me: "We know you are the last of 14 Staffel of V/(Z) LG 1. We have been expecting you for a long time, thank you!"

This book is dedicated to the memory of my fallen comrades. I hope that it will reach many of their families.

Hans-Hartmut Bechthold
Hamburg, 3 June 1996

1

Formation and the Pre-War Period

At the beginning of 1937 the Bf 109-equipped III/JG 134 was transferred from Lippstadt to Barth and was renamed II (*Schwere Jagd*) *Lehrgeschwader* with *Staffeln* 4, 5 and 6. At that time plans already existed for the unit to be equipped with the twin-engined Bf 110 then under development. The aircraft was to be used as a heavy fighter, therefore the title "*Schwere Jagd*" (heavy fighter) which appeared in brackets in the unit's designation.

At first the entire *Lehrgeschwader* was still being formed. The *Geschwader* consisted of four *Gruppen*: I (light fighter), II (heavy fighter), III (bomber) and IV (dive-bomber). In addition to Bf 109s, II *Gruppe* had available various training aircraft such as the Do 17, Fw 44, Fw 56, Fw 58 and He 70. Pilots' logbooks reveal a wide variety of flights, including airfield circuits, familiarization flights, flights in *Kette* formation, high-altitude, formation and gunnery flights, aerobatics and instrument fights as well as air combat practice, fighter training and precision and night landings. New pilots arrived as did radio operator-gunners selected for the Bf 110. The *Gruppenkommandeur* was Hptm. von Blomberg.

Toward the end of 1938 the Luftwaffe began forming a second *Lehrgeschwader*. The existing unit was renamed *Lehrgeschwader* 1, while the new one was designated *Lehrgeschwader* 2. I (Light Fighter) *Gruppe* was assigned to *Lehrgeschwader* 2. III (Bomber) and IV (Stuka) *Gruppen* remained with *Lehrgeschwader* 1 and another bomber *Gruppe* was added as II *Gruppe*. The heavy fighter (*Zerstörer*) *Gruppe*, the former II (schwere jagd) *Lehrgeschwader*, became I (schwere Jagd) *Lehrgeschwader* 1.

The first Bf 110s, which were delivered before the end of 1938, exhibited various shortcomings. The Jumo engines, modified versions of those used in the Ju 86, proved less than convincing during test flights. Corrections and improvements slowed the delivery of new machines and delayed the complete equipment of the *Gruppe* with the new type. Not until March 1939 did the Bf 110 began to rapidly replace the Bf 109. Now completely equipped with the Bf 110, on 1 June the *Gruppe* flew over Berlin during a parade. By this time Maj. Grabmann had become *Gruppenkommandeur*.

In August 1939 the *Lehrgeschwader* 1 added another bomber unit, which became I *Gruppe*. *Lehrgeschwader* 1 now consisted of three bomber *Gruppen* (I, II and III), a dive-bomber *Gruppe* (IV) and the independent heavy fighter *Gruppe*, which was now designated V *Gruppe* (*Zerstörer*) *Lehrgeschwader* 1.

Radio operator Uffz. Dierkes was one of the first members of the *Zerstörer-Gruppe* and one of the few who survived the war. The following are his recollections of the years 1938-1939:

"While at Halle Georg Lämmel and I were joined by another Georg, Georg Solluch. He was taken into our association and we became an inseparable threesome. We went through thick and thin for each other. We also concerned ourselves with the question of what was to become of us after we had served our time with the armed forces. We had signed up for 12 years. Each of us had a strength and so we were able to help one another. There were practice alerts: everyone fall out! Mad confusion. Three minutes later a neat row in front of the quarters. All the officers appeared. The chief came. Orders were issued: everyone prepare at once to move. We packed our civilian things and took them to the clothing stores. The quarters were sealed. All necessary items of equipment were packed into the assigned aircraft. The aircraft took off in the practiced sequence. Flight orders and radio frequencies were issued down at the hangar. Takeoff in 15 minutes: destination: Dresden-Klotsche, alternate airfield: any airfield around Dresden. It sank in. I could never have imagined that one could pack all his things in so short a time, change, run to the hangar, receive frequencies and flight orders, climb into the aircraft and really be able to take off in a quarter of an hour. But it was so. True we had practiced it often enough in the past, but it had never been that critical as we could cheat a little. If someone actually forgot his kit with the Knemeyer, course triangle and all his maps, someone else would always quickly help him out and everything would be all right. But today everyone had to have his things 100% in order. What a miracle. Everything was as it was supposed to be. A good performance. At Dresden-Klotsche there was a situation briefing: the supposed enemy was marching into the Reich from the east in the direction of Prague and had deployed air units to support his ground forces. As a heavy fighter unit with the Bf 110 our mission was to drive away the attacking fighters, prevent the bombers from dropping their bombs, and engage the ground forces. For this purpose our machines were armed with a new ammunition mix: 1 tracer, 1 SSmK, 1 phosphorous. But there was no action and the aircraft were left sitting with their dangerous ammunition loads. But we were kept on constant alert. At all times at least half of the crews had to be ready to take off within five minutes and the rest in fifteen minutes. We sat in deck chairs next to our machines the whole day long and we were only driven by car to the mess to eat. There was also a brief interruption for a weather briefing and the issuing of new secret radio tables. When it was all over we learned what was going on: the German armed forces had occupied the Sudetenland and a part of Czechoslovakia. And we weren't even aware of it. Fourteen days later we were back in our old routine in our garrison. That was a time in which I would often have rather turned the tables and knocked my instructor over the head, if I hadn't known that these people, whom we knew as affable from daily life, were also just following orders in trying to make a smart group out of us. And so we resigned ourselves to our fate. We were always pressed for time in the morning. Everyone had to clean something somewhere after he had washed, dressed and had breakfast. Then when we fell in, suddenly: hands up! If a button was sticking out somewhere the offender was fines, as well it was cut off as in the instructor's opinion it was not needed. I would never have believed that one could leave so many buttons undone, but there were so many. Every-

thing was checked, our undershirt, our underpants, etc. The money that was collected was used for a pleasant evening together.

Since we had every second evening off, we three always went out together and were rarely apart except when one of us had duty and the others felt a mighty thirst which could be driven away by the excellent wine that was still available in abundance in the city. As a result our passion for dancing had slowly subsided. There was by no means any gluttony, but when we tried the wine for the first time and still had no idea of its enormous effect as we were a little unsteady when we returned to the barracks. But the duty officer wasn't watching all that closely.

Then there was one more summer at home to which we could surrender ourselves light-heartedly, the summer of 1939. Our most frequent destination was Zingst, a small coastal city on the Zingst Peninsula, southwest of the island of Rügen. There, too, our threesome was inseparable. Once we missed the last train and were left standing in Zingst. It was pouring rain. As a precaution the two Georgs had applied for a leave pass. I had none. What to do? There were no taxis. It was a good twelve kilometers to the air base and only a half-hour before lights out. It was an unpleasant walk in the rain. Soon the three of us were soaked to the skin. After 45 minutes Barth came into view. Only fifteen minutes more and we would be there. Completely exhausted with clothes dripping we appeared in our quarters almost exactly as the clock struck twelve and wanted to report. But the duty officer was out just then. We went to our room and waited for rounds. Meanwhile we stripped down and wrung out our good spare uniforms like old dungarees. The water from the three uniforms almost filled a bucket. When we got up the next morning in brilliant sunshine we learned that there had been no check the previous evening. And we had walked 12 kilometers in the rain just to be on time. And the two Georgs had done so voluntarily. That was true friendship."

Dierkes went on:

"In August 1939 there were more alerts. Everything we had practiced so often was put into effect. Everything was loaded up and we moved to somewhere in central Germany. Rumors swirled through the air. Everyone knew something from some reliable source and everyone said something different. Once again we cleared out of our quarters, handed in our civilian things to the clothing stores with our names on them, put on our flight suits and climbed into our aircraft. Everything was ready for takeoff. But all of a sudden the chief shut down his machine and gave the

signal to throttle back. The engines came back to idle. A
white flare rose up from the control tower: operation can-
celed! What rubbish. They had taken great pains to get
everything in order and now it had all fallen through again.
That was the general feeling. We went back to our quarters and in the evening we were allowed to go out again as
usual. This game was repeated twice more. The third time
the chief turned up everywhere and saw for himself that
the orders were being carried out to the letter. During the
flight briefing we learned what was happening. A parade
was supposed to take place near Tannenberg and our unit
was to take part. In order to avoid an overly lengthy approach, we were supposed to fly to Jesau near Königsberg.
We took off on 25 August. When we flew past the
Tannenberg monument we saw a large camp not far away.
Large tents had been erected in rows to accommodate the
troops."

The wolf's head (brown head, red tongue, on a yellow background) served as the emblem of the Zerstörergruppe as well as of the original Lehrgeschwader and the later LG 1.

The first Bf 110 B-1s to be delivered, seen at Barth-Ostsee in summer 1938. Until the summer of 1939 V/LG 1 was designated I/(schw.Jagd) LG 1 (schw.Jagd = heavy fighter).

Bf 110s of the Lehrgeschwader parked on the airfield at Barth on the Baltic Sea. Visible in the background are the airfield buildings.

Right: Summer 1938 at Barth-Ostsee. Members of the then 6 Staffel of the Lehrgeschwader (6/(schw.Jagd) LG); from the left: Lt. Busching, Oblt. Zobel, Uffz. Struwe, Uffz. Pellnat, Uffz. Lothar, Uffz. Heldt, Uffz. Brüggow and Uffz. H. Arndt.

Below: The airfield at Barth was home to a large number of various training aircraft. In the center of the photo is one of the Lehrgeschwader's Bf 110s, still wearing the swastika emblem in its original position on a white disc.

Formation flight over the Baltic coast. The aircraft still wear the old codes: "11" for 1 (later 13) Staffel, "12" for 2 (later 14) Staffel, "13" for 3 (later 15) Staffel. "11", "12" and "13" were later replaced by "H", "K" and "L".

A Staffel of the Lehrgeschwader's Zerstörergruppe over Barth. The aircraft (Bf 110 B-1) still display the very first codes used the Lehrgeschwader's II Gruppe. Instead of the two letters that later became standard (call and Staffel letter), a single number (one or two digits) appears after the fuselage Balkenkreuz.

The aircraft of the Staffelkapitän of 6 Staffel (later 3 and then 15 Staffel), Oblt. Clausen, with radio operator Fw. Reinhold. Clausen was killed during a maintenance test flight on 22/04/1940, Reinhold was killed in action on 27/09/1940.

Above and three opposite: Bf 110 B-1s of the Lehrgeschwader in the winter of 1938-39. The Bf 110 B was superseded by the Bf 110 C. The most obvious external difference was the much more prominent oil cooler intakes on the underside of the engine cowlings of the B-variant.

Right: Fw. Reinhold being helped into his flight suit. The combination of the winter flight suit with fur collar and the Bf 110 C in the background suggest that this photo was taken during the winter of 1939-40.

Below: Members of 15 Staffel of LG 1; from the left: Uffz. Brüggow, Uffz. H. Arndt, Fw. Warrelmann, Uffz. Kramp, Obfw. Wagner, Uffz. Heldt. Only Brüggow and Warrelmann survived 1940 and the war.

2

Poland

Dierkes:

"Then came 1 September 1939. We were placed on alert at four in the morning. Our *Staffelkapitän*, Oblt. Müller, appeared wearing a very serious face and told us that the *Führer* was going to speak on the radio. In the middle of the night? We still suspected nothing. Several people suggested that it might have something to do with the border incidents and that we would now retaliate. But then our eyes were opened: war!!! We were so excited that we could scarcely eat a bite at breakfast. We sat feverishly in our quarters and waited for the order to take off. Not until 9 AM did our chief arrive with the takeoff orders. We climbed quickly into our machines. The target was Warsaw, fighter escort for He 111s of II/LG 1. In addition: defend against the enemy air force and suppress the flak batteries in and around Warsaw. If we had sufficient ammunition, on the flight home we were to place the rail line to the north under fire and hinder military transports. We were supposed to shoot at the locomotives only. Takeoff was at 9:30 AM. My insides were in turmoil. We had been flying for twenty minutes already and still nothing had happened. There, down below, the border. Now it must begin. Yes, far ahead and 1,000 meters below us several small dots. They were enemy fighters (PZL 24). They were not especially fast and we were equal to them in a turn. Our firepower was better. But could we fly better? My pilot Datz was an experienced Feldwebel. No sooner had we closed with the gaggle when all hell broke loose. As radio operator, it was my job to protect the machine against enemy attacks from behind. But now, suddenly, the enemy fighters were nowhere to be seen. Wasn't that one behind our tail? No, it was just another member of our own flight. Then there was a clattering up front in the machine. A fighter had shot at us from beneath and we hadn't even seen him. Our crate had taken several hits but otherwise everything was all right. The engines ran smoothly and neither of us was wounded."

That afternoon (4:50 – 6:50 PM) a free chase mission was flown into the Warsaw-Modlin area. No missions were flown on 2 September on account of bad weather.

Three aircraft were lost during the course of the first mission on 3 September (7:15 – 10:10 AM). Polish fighters shot down two Bf 110s of 15 *Staffel* (Uffz. Mazurowski/Uffz. Lothar and Uffz. Plankenhorn/Gefr. Kottman) and one of 14 *Staffel* (Uffz. Lindemann/Uffz. Radeck) in the Warsaw area. While the first two aircraft crashed with their crews, Uffz. Lindemann succeeded in making a forced landing near the River Bug.

Lindemann and Radek described their experience in the following report made in 1939:

"We were pursued and shot up by three Polish fighters; on fire, we had to come down just beyond the River Bug. The farmers who had watched us land came running with sticks. We fled into a swampy alder wood and stayed there until evening. In the twilight we spotted a man on horse riding along the edge of the forest. They searched for us during the night. Farmers came with dogs, clubs and old shotguns and scoured the entire wood. They had torches and poked into the bushes with long poles. We lay hidden in the rushes and were able to observe everything.

Foreground, from the left: Fw. Lindemann with his radio operator Uffz. Radeck, of 14 Staffel. On 02/09/39 the pair made a forced landing after their aircraft was damaged in combat and it took them six days to reach their own lines. This photo was taken following their return to the Gruppe.

But even the dogs could not sniff us out. We shook all night, but not from the cold. Then we moved on, through a desert of sand in which we sank up to our ankles, through moors and forests, past the villages. We came upon infantry trenches and slept in half-buried dugouts from the war. A few times, when we crawled into haystacks for the night, the next morning we were almost discovered by farmers and only managed to save ourselves at the last minute by fleeing. We had taken nothing with us, neither to eat nor drink, and so we were hungry but especially thirsty. We drank the stinking water from a flax frame. We dug holes in the marshy ground with our hands, squeezed out the moisture and let it drip into our mouths. We found almost nothing to eat and so we chewed leaves. It was very cold at night and we slept pressed close together in order to keep each other warm. On the fifth night of our flight we came to a stream in between the fronts. We squatted in the undergrowth and did knee-bends in an attempt to limber up our stiff limbs. Then we encountered Polish refugees. It was pitch-dark, no moon in the sky, and we could not see as far as the next tree trunk. We walked straight into a woman. She cried out and cursed so loudly that she woke the entire camp. We ran straight through as fast as our legs would carry us, and they ran after us, some with lanterns, but we escaped again. On the sixth day of our flight we reached our own lines. One day later we were back with our *Gruppe*, where we received a warm welcome."

The second mission on 3 September (2:35 – 5:10 PM) was into the Ploch-Ciechanow-Siercec area. During a dogfight with PZL 24s Uffz. Rahlfs, the radio operator of 13 *Staffel's Kapitän* Oblt. Müller, received a fatal head wound. Uffz. Dierkes:

"Why was our chief waggling his crate so? He moved into second place. Something wasn't right. After landing we learned what it was. A fighter had hit the chief with a well-aimed burst and had got his radio operator, Uffz. Walter Rahlfs. He must have been killed instantly. The first member of our *Staffel* to be killed in this war."

The *Gruppe* flew 16 more missions until 17 September, escort missions for bomber and Stuka units. On 7 September the deputy *Gruppenkommandeur* and *Kapitän* of 15 *Staffel*, Hptm. Schleif, and his radio operator Uffz. Haupp were killed. Their machine crashed in flames near Deblin, probably after being hit by anti-aircraft fire.

3

Phoney War

After operations in Poland ended the *Gruppe* was transferred to Würzburg, where it remained until the end of February 1940. The time was used for further training, such as instrument flying. Half of the crews were kept at readiness stations. They remained near their machines and pursued various activities to pass the time.

In December, while practicing low-flying and air combat, Fw. Stern of 13 *Staffel* struck a ferry cable over the Neckar River. Fw. Stern and his radio operator Uffz. Tietz were unable to free themselves from their crashed aircraft. Uffz. Dierkes:

"But our constant practicing was not without consequences. Shortly before Christmas the entire *Gruppe* was practicing low flying. We repeatedly flew up the Main and Neckar valleys. Of course we old hands knew where all the obstacles were. For example, there were several ferries whose cables passed straight across the river. These were dangerous things. If one came too close to one such cable while flying low there was little chance of avoiding it if one was unprepared for it. And that is what happened during one flight when the chief was flying as flight leader. The chief just managed to get his machine over the cable and the next one also just made it, but the third and last got it. The cable cut straight through the canopy, which was made of plexiglas. Four days later we carried two comrades from the air base. The radio operator was Walther Tietz from Hamburg, the pilot *Feldwebel* Stern."

Only days later two Bf 110s of 13 *Staffel* collided over Randersacker during air combat practice. Only Oblt. Glienke was able to parachute to safety, and he sustained a compound fracture of the leg. His radio operator Uffz. Landrock and the second crew, Fw. Kinzler and Obgefr. Möller, did not survive. Dierkes:

"Then on 4 January came the accident that made a deep impression on us all. Grant yourself something even when you are in trouble, for what do you have of life, if you are already dead.

A simple saying, but for me it has a deep meaning. On 1 January 1940 a comrade, Uffz. Willi 'Adele' Landrock, wrote me a postcard with this saying from his leave. His life was entirely built on this saying. How often we tried to slow him down when he once again went too far. 'Adele's' leave ended on 4 January 1940. He returned right on time. We were supposed to fly in the afternoon, air combat practice. We received our assignments during the briefing. He was off. For several days I had been plagued with a toothache. 'Adele' was assigned as replacement and had to fly in my place. When I returned from the dentist's in Würzburg I learned that two machines had crashed during air combat practice. Suspecting the worst, I learned that my machine was one of the ones that had crashed. Several days later we buried our 'Adele' and two other comrades with military honors in the city cemetery in Würzburg. Since that time I have taken a different view of that saying.

At the beginning of March we moved to Mannheim. At first the old routine continued there. We noted one small difference. Previously we were driven to the base and could eat in the mess. Now our food was brought out to us. We walked around all day in our flight suits and read whatever was available. When another *Staffel* of our *Gruppe* took over the alert watch we returned to our normal activities with small-caliber shooting, sports and other useful things. In April there was a uniform inspection parade, during which all names had to be absent from our clothes etc. Of course this had formerly been the case, but one just took along the uniform that could be shown to parade. But now this was a complete inspection. The labels even had to be cut out of our leather boots. True there was little danger that someone would take off while wearing leather boots, but better to play safe."

The former Lt. Gaffal described a mission flown by 13 *Staffel* during this period (26 March 1940):

"A reconnaissance aircraft had been tasked to watch over the area of the Rhine-Rhone canal. Our *Staffel* took the reconnaissance aircraft into its midst at the agreed-upon spot, just inside the Reich border, at an altitude of approximately 4,000 meters. At first this was no difficult job. But unnoticed by us, a numerically superior formation of Curtisses had placed itself in position to attack from out of the sun. The attack was followed by a wild dogfight with little result. When I attacked a Curtiss I came under heavy fire from another Curtiss from below. In the swirl of the dogfight neither my radio operator Uffz. Petry nor I noticed that this machine might be in a good position to attack us. While I shot down the Curtiss I fired at, I am still sure of it to this day, we were hit by a tremendous salvo. The right engine quit, I heard Petry cry out over the intercom, and he advised me that he had been badly wounded. I executed a split-S and pulled out at about 80 meters above the ground. Flying on one engine, I set course for the designated medical airfield at Trier. But that was still a flight of approximately 150 kilometers over enemy territory. Petry was still conscious and stayed in contact with me via the intercom. When we overflew the French frontier fortifications we came under heavy anti-aircraft fire, but we emerged unscathed. After a heavy landing at Trier at about 12 PM, Petry and I were rushed to the nearby hospital. The extraordinarily great loss of blood had severely weakened Petry, but he remained conscious and alert the whole time. As I had the same blood group as Petry, a transfusion was carried out at once and then the operation began. Two projectiles from the burst fired from below had pierced Petry's seat-type parachute. These bullets, which could be felt and seen beneath the skin of his belly, were lodged near his navel. During the operation it was found that the intestines had been perforated in several places and the surgeon expressed little hope to me that

Petry would survive. Petry died at approximately 4 PM without having regained consciousness. There were more than 120 bullet holes in my machine. I myself was very lucky: the heel of my right flying boot and the right leg of my flight suit had been shot through. Petry was buried on 30 March in the local cemetery of his home town of Ballersbach in the presence of his comrades."

Two other machines sustained serious damage on that 26 March. Their engines shot up, Fw. Datz and Uffz. Lämmel had to make a wheels-up landing in a field near Lutzerath. Apart from bruises they were uninjured. Fw. Warrelmann and Uffz. Kramp only made it as far as Mainz/Mombach after their aircraft lost all its coolant as a result of battle damage.

On 29 March the aircraft of Fw. Lindemann and Uffz. Radek was hit by anti-aircraft fire near Waldhausen, 10 kilometers north of Bitsch, during a high-altitude weapons test. Fw. Lindemann bailed out of the crashing Bf 110 and was captured by the French with serious arm injuries. Uffz. Radek failed to get out of the cockpit.

The crew of Lt. Busching and Uffz. Arndt of 15 *Staffel* was killed on 2 April. The *Gruppe* was attacked by French fighters in the Nancy-Hagenau area while escorting a reconnaissance machine. After successfully fighting off the attack, the Bf 110s had to climb up through a thick layer of cloud. The *Gruppe* became separated in cloud and each flew home alone. Not until all the aircraft had landed was the loss of Lt. Busching and Uffz. Arndt realized.

On 22 April the *Kapitän* of 15 *Staffel*, Oblt. Clausen, was killed in an accident. In 1993 Gaffal (then a *Leutnant* in 13 *Staffel*) wrote:

"At the time in question V/LG 1 was stationed at Mannheim-Sandhofen airfield, where it was kept in a state of constant readiness. 13 *Staffel*, to which I belonged, was at the dispersal, laying about in deck chairs bored stiff and playing with the *Staffel* dogs.

From my deck chair I watched as Oblt. Clausen, coming from the repair shop, taxied out for takeoff. I had to assume that it was a maintenance test flight, which was later confirmed. Clausen was completely alone at an altitude of about 1,200 meters over the airfield, carrying out several flight maneuvers which I watched attentively from my deck chair. Suddenly I realized that the aircraft was now flying on just one engine, it must have had an engine failure. I now watched as he began the landing maneuver, completely unconcerned because all of us pilots had mastered landing on one engine. Furthermore Clausen was a very experienced pilot. Now standing, I watched the landing approach, which began absolutely flawlessly. When

Clausen was at about 50 meters above the runway, I noticed with horror that part of the herd of sheep on the airfield was on the runway. Clausen must have now seen this too, for he tried to go around from a height of about 10 meters. While the machine cleared the herd of sheep, it was unable to gain sufficient height to get over the houses of Sandhofen, which lay right off the departure end of the runway. The aircraft was fully fueled and fully armed, and therefore was at maximum takeoff weight. Both wings were torn off in the following collision with houses, the aircraft's fuselage crashed into a street and skidded along it for about 200 meters. The loss of the wings caused the fuel tanks to empty their contents over the houses and into the street. Not until all of the ammunition had exploded could the bodies of Clausen and the mechanic who was with him be removed from the fuselage. Tragically, at the time of the impact a young woman with a baby carriage stepped out of one of the houses that was set on fire and was doused in gasoline. Both she and her child sustained fatal burns. My comrades and I who observed the incident were certain that Clausen wanted to avoid landing into the herd of sheep and so had begun the overshoot maneuver. It was certainly a spontaneous reaction, as there was no time for reflection. The *Kommandeur* assigned me the sad task of driving to Sandhofen in the early evening and expressing our *Gruppe's* deepest regrets to the mayor."

The next day the *Staffel*, under the command of Clausen's radio operator Fw. Reinhold, bade a military farewell to Clausen before the doors of the train that was to take him home to Husum closed.

On 30 April Oblt. Schnoor, who came from I/ZG 52, took over 15 *Staffel* as *Kapitän*. On 16 April *Gruppenkommandeur* Maj. Grabmann had handed V/LG 1 over to Hptm. Liensberger, who also came from I/ZG 52. Maj. Grabmann became *Kommodore* of ZG 76 (II and III *Gruppen*).

Far left Fw. Jecke, then Fw. Datz with radio operator Uffz. Lämmel; behind them is Fw. Schob, who was transferred to ZG 76 on 18/03/1940 and survived the war, finishing up with the rank of Hauptmann. At the time the photo was taken all were members of 13 Staffel; Jecke was later transferred to 14 Staffel.

15 Staffel at readiness stations; from the left: Uffz. Maresch, Uffz. Kramp, Uffz. Lochow – all three were killed over England in 1940.

Below: Mannheim: members of 13 Staffel take their midday meal in the open air. Far left: Staffelkapitän Oblt. Müller, Lt. Gaffal, Fw. Kobert, Uffz. Lämmel, Fw. Hoffmann, on the inside of the table Fw. Datz and Obfw. Stegemann.

Servicing and repair work at the workshops in Mannheim. With the exception of one aircraft (L1+YB, adjutant Oblt. Zobel), all belong to 13 Staffel (last letter of the aircraft code "H", third – call – letter in white). All except L1+YB ("B" indicated the Gruppe's headquarters, or Stab) have dark green upper surfaces and sides with pale blue under surfaces. The fuselage sides of L1+YB have been oversprayed in pale blue, leaving just the upper fuselage, wings and tail in dark green. Both camouflage schemes were seen during the campaign against France in 1940. Apparently some machines were resprayed (several times) while others were not, however dark-painted fuselage sides were still seen during the Battle of Britain.

Waiting for the order to take off. 13 Staffel; from the left: Obfw. Schob, Uffz. Pape, Uffz. Klever, Fw. Kobert, Uffz. Landrock, Uffz. Dierkes, Uffz. Schäfer, Uffz. Petry, Uffz. Lämmel.

An aircraft of 15 Staffel (L1+LL) flown by the crew of Oblt. Weckeiser and Uffz. Brüggow.

Bf 110s of 15 Staffel over Mannheim. The aircraft call letters (here "C", "A" and "B") were yellow.

Right: Members of 15 Staffel playing cards; from the left: Fw. Warrelmann, Uffz. Brüggow, Obfw. Wagner, Fw. Reinhold, Oblt. Zobel.

Oblt. Müller, Staffelkapitän of 13 Staffel (left) and Lt. Gaffal on the airfield at Mannheim.

Obfw. Stegemann and Lt. Gaffal of 13 Staffel check to make sure that labels and names on clothing which might include the name of the unit or give some clue to it are removed as per regulations. From the left: Fw. Datz, Fw. Kobert, Fw. Krone, Fw. Hoffmann, Uffz. Pape, Uffz. Petry, Uffz. Solluch, Uffz. Lämmel, Uffz. Dierkes – Obfw. Stegemann and Lt. Gaffal – Fw. Krone. Krone displays his opinion of this action by sticking out his tongue. He was Major Grabmann's radio operator and was killed shortly after the two were transferred to ZG 76 (of which Grabmann was Kommodore) in May 1940. Grabmann was able to parachute to safety.

Oblt. Glienke points in the direction of the photographer. He must have said something amusing, as Fw. Kobert and Obfw. Stegemann (left) are laughing. On the extreme right is Lt. Gaffal.

Left: Three Feldwebel of 13 Staffel; from the left: Fw. Hoffmann (radio operator of Staffelkapitän Oblt. Müller), Obfw. Stegemann and Fw. Kobert. Right: Fw. Krone always seemed to be making jokes, including here during a lecture by 13 Staffel. From the left: Uffz. Dierkes, Fw. Kobert, Fw. Datz, Uffz. Pape, Fw. Jentzsch, Obfw. Stegemann, Fw. Meinig, Fw. Hoffmann, Fw. Krone.

Fw. Kobert, Obfw. Stegemann and Uffz. Solluch during a game of skat. Perhaps this is another reason why this period was referred to as the "Sitzkrieg" (sitting war).

Above and below: Bf 110s of I/ZG 52 over southern Germany, early 1940. The unit was renamed II/ZG 2 at the beginning of June and took part in the operations over Great Britain as such. The unit code "A2" remained the same. Hptm. Liensberger came to V/(Z)LG 1 from I/ZG 52 in mid-April, followed several weeks later by Oblt. Schnoor.

Aircraft of I/ZG 52 during a practice flight over the Stubai Valley in Tirol.

Bf 110s of I/ZG 52 on the airfield at Kaufbeuren/Allgäu, February 1940. Second from the left Oblt. Schnoor, third Hptm. Liensberger.

Staffelkapitän of 15 Staffel, Oblt. Clausen, who was killed during a maintenance test flight on 22 April 1940.

Lt. Eisele and Oblt. Schnoor of 15 Staffel on the airfield at Mannheim.

Right: Lt. Schultze of 13 Staffel. On 17 April 1940 he was shot down in combat with French fighters. He and his radio operator Uffz. Wiebe survived the subsequent crash-landing, in which the aircraft overturned, and were temporarily prisoners of war of the French.

Below: Forced landing by Fw. Datz of 13 Staffel near Lutzerath on 26 March 1940. According to his logbook, "both engines failed."

Uffz. Petry (left) and Fw. Hoffmann. Petry, the radio operator of Lt. Gaffal of 13 Staffel, was seriously wounded in combat with French Morane fighters during a reconnaissance mission on 26 March 1940. He died in hospital the same day. A detail from his 13 Staffel attended the funeral in Petry's home town of Ballersdorf. The two photos of the gravesite were taken in the Ballersbach cemetery in 1940 and 1991.

Fw. Kinzler of 13 Staffel in his Bf 110, winter 1939-40. On 4 January 1940 he and his radio operator Obgefr. Möller were involved in a midair collision with the aircraft flown by the crew of Oblt. Glienke and Uffz. Landrock during air combat exercises over Randersacker. Glienke alone was able to parachute to safety.

4

France

On 10 May 1940 the crews went to readiness status before 5 AM as usual. Uffz. Jäckel, radio operator of Lt. Schalkhausser of 14 *Staffel*, had left his map and course plotter in his quarters. He ran to get them. When he came back the bunker was empty. From the airfield he heard the sound of engines. Jäckel ran there and saw the aircraft moving about in the darkness of the shadows. One had an open rear canopy. It was his. Schalkhausser spotted him and waved his hand. Jäckel managed to get into the moving aircraft. By the time he had strapped in and put on his oxygen mask his machine was already in the air. In this way he had nearly missed the war. For on this day the "Sitzkrieg" or "Phoney War" was over, German troops had crossed the border into France.

That day V/LG 1 flew three escort missions into the Metz-Verdun-Sedan-Neufchateau area. The crews met heavy anti-aircraft fire but no French or British fighters.

On 11 May the *Gruppe* was ordered to rendezvous with two returning bomber formations. Three times there were combats with French Curtiss fighters, however there were no losses. On the other hand the Bf 110 of Lt. Leickhardt and Uffz. Fabian was hit by flak near St. Mihiel. Only Lt. Leickhardt managed to bail out of the spinning machine. He was captured by the French and spent five months in hospital with serious leg injuries. The official casualty reported stated briefly: "Spun down in anti-aircraft fire near St. Mihiel at 7:35 AM and disappeared into cloud."

On 12 May the *Gruppe* flew two escort missions for bomber formations to Sedfan-Charleville-Mourmelon. During the first 13 *Staffel* lost three aircraft in combat with French fighters.

In 1991 Gaffal wrote:

"We took off at about 7 AM with orders to rendezvous with the homeward bound KG 53 in the approximate area of Reims-Mourmelon. The weather was very good that morning and we had a good view of the ground as we headed in at approximately 4,000 meters. Our formation flew into the assigned combat area in closed formation. We could see the aircraft of KG 53 in the area just east of Reims from a very long way off. When we neared the bombers, which were flying in very close formation, we spotted a large number of French fighters which had positioned themselves to attack KG 53. We attacked immediately and a wild dogfight broke out. I saw a Morane attacking a He 111, gave chase and was able to shoot down the Morane. During this a flight of four French fighters moved into position against me, and I was only able to evade their attack by making a split-S to ground level. My radio operator Uffz. Dierkes advised me that four Moranes were following us closely and firing constantly. With the four fighters on my tail I had no choice: roughly near Rethel I headed my machine into the Aisne Valley and set course for home at treetop height. The French flight of four split up. Two Moranes flew directly behind me and fired persistently, but they had no chance of hitting me with their fixed weapons as they had to fly just as low as I. Therefore their bursts of tracer all passed just above us. While we busied ourselves with the two Frenchmen directly behind us, the other two managed to pull abreast of us on the crest of the line of wooded hills that followed the river. In order to avoid getting into an even worse position, I decided to attack these two fighters flying to my right. I made an extremely steep right turn in an attempt to get into firing position. The French reacted immediately to this maneuver and likewise turned toward us and fired, without result. When the French had passed over me and I had rolled my machine level with the slope, I had lost so much speed that I was unable to fly over the hills, even at full throttle. On the verge of a stall, I scraped the wooded crest of the line of hills. The tail of my machine was torn off in the trees, and my Bf 110 crashed from a height of about 80 meters above a quarry beside a road at an impact angle of about fifty degrees. I was able to switch off the ignition and remove my glasses before the crash. At the time of the crash my machine was completely intact and we probably also had not been hit. The crash site was approximately 10 kilometers behind the front. I do not know how I was pulled from the machine. I woke up 27 hours later, a prisoner of the French. I has suffered a fracture at the base of the skull, an open fracture of the frontal bone and knee injuries."

Gaffal's radio operator, Uffz. Dierkes, has the following memories of this fateful day:

"We looked for the bomber formation we were supposed to cover. Far ahead it flew in peaceful formation. It did not appear to have been attacked. We flew after it at full throttle. We had almost caught up to it when my pilot Lt. Gaffal looked up and saw a single French fighters. But what was that? That was not just one but at least ten fighters circling over us in loose formation. Gaffal turned toward one machine. He did not hear my shouts. Our two wingmen should have followed us. But had they seen the other aircraft? I can no longer ask them, both were shot down. We still had not fired a shot. We tried to gain height first. When we were at the same height as the others I saw my two comrades shot down. The French turned toward us and lined up for another pass. Now it was our turn. While we fired at a fighter in front of us and were able to shoot it down, we came under heavy fire from behind. Soon all my drums of ammunition were gone, but five machines were still there. We lost height steadily. Then a road appeared in front of us at right angles to our direction of flight. We raced towards it. Would we manage to clear it or would we crash onto it? When I came to I was lying in the shattered machine. A fuel tank or the ammunition might go up at any second. My first thought was to get out fast. Something was wrong with my arm, blood dripped from my forehead into my eyes. Only one impulse motivated me: get out! I pushed the canopy jettison lever with my foot, nothing moved. But there was another lever up front and when I pushed it with my foot the canopy moved a little but did not pop off as it was supposed to. After

removing my parachute I braced my back against the middle seat, lifted my legs and pushed with all my might against the roof. I succeeded in opening a crack through which I made it onto a wing. From there I succeeded in shaking my unconscious pilot Lt. Gaffal awake for a moment and getting him out of the cockpit. Soon afterward there appeared French soldiers who took us to medics."

Both Gaffal and Dierkes returned to V/LG 1 after they were released from French captivity in July 1940. Because of his serious head injuries Gaffal was judged no longer fit to fly fighters; Dierkes flew a number of missions with the successor *Gruppe* I/NJG 3 and subsequently became an instructor, training Hungarian night fighter crews.

On 12 May the crew of Lt. Schultze and Uffz. Wiebe flew in the top cover *Schwarm* with Lt. Gaffal and Uffz. Dierkes. In 1992 Wiebe related:

"Over the border we received anti-aircraft fire and held course for Verdun. The attack *Schwarm* flew out in front. The anti-aircraft fire stopped, a sign that now fighters would appear. The first Morane showed itself. In the developing dogfight we became separated from the formation. Schultze attacked a Morane from behind. He hit it and I saw it disappear below. As a result of a loss of height of approximately 2,000 meters we were unable to find the formation. Suddenly three Curtisses positioned themselves behind us, somewhat higher. A Morane which came from behind veered off under my heavy fire. Our left engine was hit and stopped, after which one Curtiss from above and another from below tried to force us to land. Meanwhile I has expended all of my ammunition. I felt a heavy blow on my right knee and soon afterwards another one on my left knee (bullet wounds, as it later turned out). The intercom was out and the left engine was losing power. We had to go down. We made a forced landing which ended in our machine overturning. We lay trapped in our machine and hoped that it would not catch fire. We were lucky. After some time I was rescued by Frenchmen. I had no idea whether Schultze had survived, I did not see him again."

After the release of German prisoners held by the French in July, Schultze returned to the *Gruppe* for a short time. He was transferred and was killed in action on 8 January 1944 while serving with 14 *Staffel* of KG 2. After returning from a night mission over London his Me 410 crashed near Boulogne for unknown reasons. His identity disc was found at the crash site in 1962. Schultze's radio operator Uffz. Wiebe, who was shot down with him on 12 May 1940, was also released from

French captivity and returned to V/LG 1. Obviously Wiebe was unaware that his pilot Lt. Schultze had survived and returned. He continued to fly with V/LG 1 and later with the night-fighter *Gruppe* I/NJG 1 and survived the war.

The third aircraft of the covering flight from 13 *Staffel* that was shot down on 12 May was crewed by Uffz. Hartenstein and Uffz. Conrad. The crew failed to escape from their burning, spinning Bf 110.

On 13 and 14 May the *Gruppe* flew escort missions into the Verdun-Sedan-Charleville area. There were no encounters with French fighters, however anti-aircraft fire was heavy.

The crew of Lt. Schwarzer and Obgefr. Petrich of 15 *Staffel* was lost on the first of three missions flown on 16 May. They were shot down in an air battle over La Fere while escorting a reconnaissance aircraft.

The first engagement with British fighters occurred one day later on 17 May during an escort mission for He 111s of KG 2. Spitfires shot down two aircraft of 14 *Staffel* and another was obliged to make a forced landing. The Bf 110s of *Staffelkapitän* Oblt. Methfessel and his gunner Uffz. Resener and Uffz. Schmitt and Obgefr. Schmidt crashed west of Reims.

The aircraft of Lt. Schalkhausser and his radio operator Uffz. Jäckel was also hit, but this crew was luckier. Jäckel remembered:

"We were attacked by Spitfires and there was a lengthy dogfight. My pilot *Leutnant* Schalkhausser fired a few times. A Spitfire turned behind us and bullets hit us. Schalkhausser made a split-S from approximately 3,000 to 700 meters, and I was pressed into my seat when we pulled out. The right engine had stopped. We flew home at a steady height. Once we came under anti-aircraft fire, which was at the right altitude but off to our right. With one engine out the machine pulled to the right instead of flying straight. Over the Ardennes the single engine could no longer carry on. I saw a high forest pass beneath us. Where it ended there was a flat, sandy downhill slope and there Schalkhausser made a belly landing, which seemed quite smooth to me. At the end of the hill there was a stream with bushes and we roared through this. The red sand that was thrown up made me think that the aircraft was burning, but that was not the case.

Soon German soldiers and an officer came. A sticking plaster was applied to my bleeding chin, then we were driven to the nearest hospital in Arlon, I still with my parachute. The doctor in the hospital said that he would be happy if he had only minor cases like mine. He kept Schalkhausser there as he had a flesh wound in his buttocks caused by a phosphorous bullet. Because of the poisoning it took a long time for the wound to heal. I did not see him again. (Author's note: while serving with 1./ZG

76, Schalkhausser was killed in action on June 26, 1944 northeast of Vienna during a dogfight with P-51s and P-38s – six Me 410s of 1 *Staffel* were shot down.).

They told me that I should make my way to Luxembourg as there was a forward airfield there. So I tossed my parachute over my shoulder and set off. I could only walk in the ditches or along the side of the road, for the roads were clogged with advancing troops and train units. Occasionally a few comments were called my way, asking if I had lost my desire and so on. From the airfield in Luxembourg I was able to hitch a ride to Frankfurt in a Ju 52 carrying wounded and from there caught a train to Wiesbaden. I arrived there on a Sunday. I attracted some attention, and I was somewhat embarrassed to get off there, still with my parachute on my back, sweaty and dust-covered and with a few dried splashes of blood on my flight suit. The airfield was empty, occupied only by the base administration and air traffic control. At the commander's office they referred me to an information post for personnel separated from their units in Wiesbaden. There I learned that the *Gruppe* had been transferred to St. Marie in Belgium. Which of three St. Maries they could not tell me. Back at the commander's office they decided that I should fly to Sedan in a Ju 52 the next day. The aircraft was taking ammunition there and was supposed to fly over the three St. Maries on the flight back. So the next day we took off, the pilot, the copilot and I, behind crates of ammunition, below in the Pfalz columns and vehicles on all the roads. After the Ju had landed we flew back and stopped at the first St. Marie. There were Bf 110s there, but not ours. We didn't even land at the second St. Marie. There were also Bf 110s there, but with different noses. Furthermore the pilot did not want to fly any more because evening was approaching. Therefore I flew back again. They told me that I should report to the airfield commander's office every day, because the *Gruppe* still had articles there that would be picked up in the next few days. Therefore I reported each day and somehow managed to kill the rest of the day. One day two trucks came from the *Gruppe*. My comrades were more than a little taken aback to find me there. Naturally Lt. Schalkhausser and I had already been written off by the *Gruppe*. We drove back to St. Marie and then there was another big hullabaloo when I reappeared on the scene."

In 1987 Maj. Grabmann, as of mid-April 1940 *Kommodore* of ZG 76 (II and III *Gruppen*), previously *Kommandeur* of V/LG 1, wrote of his experience on that 17th May:

"I got it near Dinant while leading a *Staffel* of Bf 110s escorting a unit of Do 17 bombers making low-level attacks. We ran into British fighters. In air combat at low level the Bf 110 was unable to bring to bear the superiority it enjoyed at altitude. My machine took a hit which rendered it incapable of maneuvering. I had to bail out at a height of 600 meters and my parachute opened just in time just above the ground. That was near Cambrai. French anti-aircraft gunners took me prisoner and brought me to the jail in Cambrai. The next day I and all the inmates of the prison were marched off in the direction of Amiens. On the way we were overtaken by German tanks and they immediately took me along with them. I accompanied them on their unopposed advance to the Channel coast. I stayed there for almost a week until the opportunity presented itself to fly in a Do 17 reconnaissance aircraft back to my last base at Dinant, where I found my staff. It looked as if, for me, the entire war was already over after only seven days. When I landed at Dinant I met the corps commander General Grauert. I made no bones about the fact that I considered fighter escort for bombers making low-level attacks to be madness, because our fighters and *Zerstörer* had no room to maneuver against the slower British Hurricane and French Morane fighters and were therefore at a considerable disadvantage."

Oblt. Müntefering, formerly of the *Gruppenstab* (technical officer), replaced the fallen Oblt. Methfessel as *Kapitän* of 14 *Staffel*. He flew his last mission with V/LG 1 on 13 July 1940, then he joined the night-fighters, III/NJG 1 (7 *Staffel*). On 13 March 1941 his Bf 110 was shot down by German fighters during a night mission. The position of technical officer was left vacant. Along with *Major* Grabmann, who took over as *Kommodore* of ZG 76 on 16 April, the unit also lost *Gruppenadjutant* Oblt. Thimmig, who was succeeded by Oblt. Zobel of 15 *Staffel*.

As of 13 May the *Gruppe* flew several times from Mannheim-Sandhofen to airfields nearer the France-Luxembourg border: on the 13th to Wiesbaden, on the 17th to Wengerohr and on the 19th to Trier. A further move forward followed on the 20th, for the first time across the border to Belgium. The new base was St. Marie, where the *Gruppe* was to remain until 28 June. The small town lay several kilometers east of Libramont and north of Neufchateau. Sleeping quarters were in the town, where the crews were housed in private houses and also in a school. Each day trucks drove them to the airfield. The time was based on the missions to be flown. Blockhouses and tents erected on the airfield served as workshop buildings, ready rooms and kitchens. Sometimes food was also bought in the town.

The *Gruppe* flew 31 more missions, mainly bomber escort, before hostilities in France ceased on 25 June:

18 May:	Charleville-Reims-Compiegne, second mission: Amiens-Abbeville
19 May:	Epernay-Compiegne, air combat with French fighters
20 May:	Moutidier-Soissons, air combat with Moranes
21 May:	Amiens-Pontoise, air combat with French fighters; Obfw. Stegemann and Uffz. Solluch of 13 *Staffel* were killed while taking off from St. Marie. It is believed that the elevators jammed, causing the machine to crash on to the airfield boundary from a height of only about 100 meters.
23 May:	St. Quentin-St. Omer-Aras-Cambrai
24 May:	Beauvais-Amiens, air combat with Spitfires
25 May:	Beauvais-Amiens, second mission: Clermont-Amiens-St. Quentin, air combat with French fighters; third mission: Amiens-St. Quentin, air combat.
26 May:	Arras-Amiens-Beauvais-Le Havre; second mission: Lagny-Paris
27 May:	Liege-Ostende-Dunkirk, air combat with Spitfires; second mission: Arras-Dunkirk, air combat with Spitfires.
28 May:	Amiens
29 May:	Amiens
01 June:	Arlon
03 June:	Amiens-Paris
06 June:	Reims-Meuny-Paris
07 June:	Two missions to Clermont
09 June:	Rethel
10 June:	Rethel-Vouziers; second mission: Reims-Epernay
11 June:	Eperney-Charlons; second mission: Rethel-Reims
12 June:	Rethel-Revigny-Bar le Duc
14 June:	Epinal-Toul
15 June:	Verdun-Epinal-Vesoul; second mission: Verdun-Epinal-Toul
16 June:	Rethel.

While the *Gruppe's* losses during the first eight days of operations against France totaled 8 aircraft with 9 aircrew killed and 7 wounded, most seriously, during the period from 18 May until 16 June – the day of its last mission against the French – the unit did not suffer any more casualties in air combat.

There was a general rest break from 17 to 26 June. Several aircraft went to Würzburg or Mannheim for overhaul or were replaced by new machines. Personnel went on rest and recreation outings to Antwerp and Liege.

Force-landed French machine (Potez). It appears that several sections of the canopy have already been removed.

Uffz. Brüggow (standing) smiles at his "black man" (Luftwaffe slang for a mechanic). On the right, next to Brüggow, is Uffz. Maresch, also of 15 Staffel.

Aircraft of Fw. Datz of 13 Staffel (L1+JH). The saplings in the foreground were used to camouflage the aircraft and here have already been removed from the Bf 110.

Fw. Schob, Fw. Kobert, Obfw. Stegemann and Fw. Hoffmann, all of 13 Staffel. In the background is an aircraft of 14 Staffel (L1+EK). The third letter in the aircraft code (the call letter), in this case an "E", was red with a white outline on 14 Staffel aircraft. 13 Staffel had white letters, 15 Staffel yellow (no outline).

Zerstörergruppe

On 13 May 1940 Uffz. Bechthold (radio operator Uffz. Harder) of 14 Staffel overran the airfield at Mannheim after returning from a mission. Bechthold remembers the "dismay" of the workshop foreman, as the machine had just been completely overhauled. In the center of the photo is the shop foreman, to his right Uffz. Harder and Uffz. Bechthold.

15 Staffel; from the left: Fw. Warrelmann, Uffz. Lothar, Uffz. H. Arndt, Uffz. Heldt, Fw. Reinhold and Uffz. Brüggow.

Left: Two old friends from the Barth days, Uffz. Heldt and Uffz. Brüggow of 15 Staffel.

Staffelkapitän of 14 Staffel, Oblt. Methfessel; he was killed on 17 May 1940.

Members of an army unit check the papers of Lt. Schalkhausser and Uffz. J. Jäckel of 14 Staffel following their forced landing near Arlon on 17 May 1940. Interest in the two airmen appears to have been great.

The aircraft of Oblt. Weckeiser and radio operator Uffz. Brüggow (L1+LL) photographed from another 15 Staffel aircraft. The letter "I" may be seen on the aircraft's wing in the foreground. L1+IL was flown by Lt. Altendorf (radio operator Uffz. W. Arndt).

Left: The letter "A" is visible on this aircraft's wingtip, identifying it as L1+AH, the aircraft of Lt. Gaffal of 13 Staffel, seen here in the machine's cockpit. Right: The old standard (1./Zerstörer) was also seen at St. Marie; it belonged to 13 Staffel, which had evolved from 1 Staffel (schwere Jagd)/LG 1. The Gruppe's official stamp was never changed. Even V/(Z)LG 1's last loss report dated 27 September 1940 is stamped "Stab/I. (s.Jagd) Lehrgeschwader 1."

Left: St. Marie near Libramont in Belgium. V/LG 1 was based not far from this village from 20 to 28 May 1940. The crews were billeted in homes in the village. Right: The command post and quarters of the Stab of V/LG 1.

The Staffelkapitän usually flew an aircraft with the call letter (first letter after the Balkenkreuz) "A". The aircraft depicted here, L1+AL, was probably that of the Staffelkapitän of 15 Staffel. Visible above the "AL" is the tail of another Bf 110 positioned to this aircraft's left.

L1+EH, the aircraft of Obfw. Stegemann and his radio operator Uffz. Solluch of 13 Staffel. On 21 May 1940, one day after the unit had moved to the forward airfield at St. Marie, the aircraft crashed shortly after takeoff for reasons unknown. Since Obfw. Stegemann was one of the Gruppe's longest-serving and most experienced pilots, rumors began to circulate as to the cause of the crash: sabotage or perhaps faulty maintenance or technical failure (elevator)? The crew were buried near the crash site.

Personnel of 13 Staffel inspect a Fairey Battle light bomber of the RAF which force-landed near Bouillon (only a few kilometers from the unit's airfield at St. Marie) on 11 May 1940. Since the Gruppe did not move to St. Marie until 20 May, this inspection had to have taken place weeks after the forced landing. Several pieces have already been removed from the wreck, and a bird has already made a nest in the tail section, in front of which is seen Uffz. Seufert. In front of, on or beside the machine are, beginning 2nd from the left: Oblt. Glienke, Uffz. Dieckmann, Uffz. Weller, Oblt. Müller, Fw. Jentzsch, Lt. Beck.

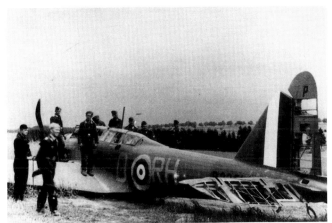

"Construction work" on the perimeter of the forward airfield. In the background is L1+AK, the machine of the Staffelkapitän of 14 Staffel.

Oblt. Fenske of 14 Staffel. He was transferred to III/NJG 2 on 21 July 1940 and was killed in action on 26 March 1944 while serving with NJG 10.

Members of 15 Staffel engaged in "construction work" at St. Marie; from the left: Uffz. Lochow, Uffz. Maresch, unidentified, Uffz. Hamann and Uffz. Meinhard.

Above: Ground personnel of 15 Staffel (right) with three radio operators; from the left: Uffz. Heidrich, Uffz. Maresch and Uffz. Brüggow.

Above right: Uffz. Arndt, radio operator of Lt. Altendorf of 15 Staffel, on a captured British motorcycle (BSA) in front of his Staffel's quarters.

Right: In the center is Uffz. Lochow, to his right Uffz. Meinhard and Uffz. Hamann, all of 15 Staffel.

Below: This Ju 87 Stuka made an emergency landing on V/LG 1's airfield at St. Marie.

Above and right: 15 Staffel's mess hut, camouflaged with spruce boughs. Unit personnel after mail call. Fourth from the left is Uffz. Brüggow, beside him his pilot Oblt. Weckeiser. Kneeling beside Weckeiser is Uffz. Pfaffelhuber.
Below: Sometimes personnel also got together for a game of cards at St. Marie. From the left: Oblt. Schnoor, Oblt. Weckeiser (15 Staffel).

The aircraft of Oblt. Weckeiser and radio operator Uffz. Brüggow of 15 Staffel in May-June 1940. Brüggow's comment: "On the forward airfield at St. Marie after returning from a combat mission. We rolled over a harrow and got a flat tire. Ergo head-stand, fortunately the aircraft did not overturn."

Three Bf 110s of 15 Staffel, L1+IL (the "I" is visible on the upper surface of the wing), L1+HL and L1+FL. Note that the fuselage sides and vertical tail of L1+HL are finished in a light camouflage color with a soft mottle, while the same surfaces on L1+FL are finished in a dark color.

Above: Paperwork for members of 15 Staffel; left Oblt. Schnoor.

Right: The crew of Fw. Jecke and radio operator Uffz. Harder of 14 Staffel. Harder had previously flown with Uffz. Bechthold, then Jecke and eventually with Fw. Würgatsch, with whom he was killed in a failed forced landing on 21 July 1940.

Fw. Jecke in front of his L1+BK (14 Staffel). It is obvious that the aircraft's factory code (Stammkennzeichen) has been overpainted; as well, the white surround of the fuselage Balkenkreuz has been narrowed. This aircraft is also finished in the dark green camouflage scheme.

Aircraft parked in or near the edge of the forest which bordered the forward airfield at St. Marie. On the extreme right is a tarpaulin-covered Bf 108, which was used as a communications aircraft, on the left a Bf 110 of 13 Staffel coded L1+. H. From the left: Kommandeur Hptm. Liensberger, mechanic, Oblt. Schnoor (15 Staffel), medical officer, Oblt. Haarmann (special duties officer).

Above: The raising of glasses suggests that 13 Staffel must have had some-thing to celebrate. From the left: Lt. Gorisch, Oblt. Glienke, Lt. Beck, Oblt. Müller. None of these men survived September 1940.

Right: The aircraft of the Gruppenkommandeur, L1+XB.

Below: Oblt. Müller, the Staffelkapitän of 13 Staffel, uses his hands to recreate a combat. From the left: Ordnance Sergeant Knuth, Oblt. Müntefering (Tech-nical Officer, later Staffelkapitän of 14 Staffel), Hptm. Liensberger (Kommandeur), Oblt. Braun (special duties officer), Oblt. Zobel (adjutant, later Staffelkapitän 14 Staffel), Oblt. Müller (Staffelkapitän of 13 Staffel and 1 Staffel that preceded it).

Obfw. Wagner with his radio operator Uffz. Heldt (15 Staffel) in the shadow of their Bf 110.

Right: Fw. Datz of 13 Staffel with unit mascot at readiness near his L1+JH. Datz was shot down in this machine over the English Channel on 13 August 1940; he returned from Canada, where he was held as a prisoner of war, in 1946.

Below: Workshop company at work at St. Marie, repairing or replacing an engine.

Lt. Altendorf in front of Bf 110s of his 15 Staffel.

Aircraft of 15 Staffel over Cherbourg, with the fort visible in the background. The aircraft in the center of the photo is L1+AL.

Left: How fast-moving were those times, with the fates of men decided in days, weeks at most. From the left: Obfw. Wagner (killed on 13/08/40), Oblt. Schnoor (transferred to night fighters, survived the war), Oblt. Weckeiser (shot down on 27/09/40, POW), all of 15 Staffel. Right: From the left: Oblt. Weckeiser, Lt. Eisele, Oblt. Schnoor, Obfw. Wagner, all of 15 Staffel.

15 Staffel taking a meal. Second from the left is Fw. Reinhold.

Lt. Becker of 14 Staffel acting as "construction foreman."

Above: Bf 110s of 15 Staffel.

Right: Uffz. Bechthold of 14 Staffel at the controls of his Bf 110; the head of his radio operator Uffz. Koch is just visible in the left foreground. Often photos such as this were taken by the radio operator, who ducked down and took a picture with the camera held high.

Below: The Stab dispersal, surrounded by small trees stuck into the ground. In the background is L1+XB, the aircraft of Hptm. Liensberger.

L1+YB, the aircraft of Oblt. Zobel, the adjutant. The letter "B" signified the Stab of a First Gruppe. The Fifth Gruppe in question should have carried a "G" for the Stab. As well the Staffel code (fourth letter) should have been "X", "Y", "Z" for a Fifth Gruppe instead of "H", "K", "L" for a First Gruppe. But nothing was changed and instead the new V Gruppe retained the code letters of the former I Gruppe. This even irritated the British, as a declassified document confirms (RAF Secret Intelligence Report 28/1940 – V/Lehrgeschwader).

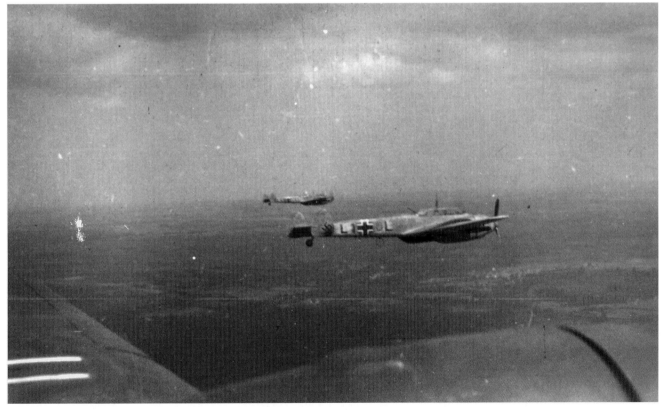

Aircraft of 15 Staffel. The nearest aircraft is either L1+DL or L1 +BL.

Above: 15 Staffel takes lunch. Second from the left is Obfw. Wagner, first from the right Oblt. Weckeiser, beside him Lt. Eisele.

Right: Hptm. Liensberger with the repair company; in the background on the right is Oblt. Braun, special duties officer.

Below: Mechanic on the cockpit sill of Hptm. Liensberger's L1+XB. The aircraft is also identifiable (as a Stab aircraft) by its propeller spinner tip (one-third white, two-thirds green). 13 Staffel aircraft had white spinner tips, 14 Staffel red and 15 Staffel yellow.

Although this Bf 110 has been camouflaged with several birch trees, their value is questionable on this exposed field.

L1+GL of 15 Staffel. This aircraft displays a variety of finishes, with pale, lightly-mottled fuselage sides and a dark overspray on the fin and rudder.

Left: Servicing and aligning the aft-firing machine-gun of a Bf 110 (MG 15, 7.92-mm). Right: V/LG 1 receives a visit from two Messerschmitt engineers (on the right); from the left: Oblt. Haarmann (special duties officer), Hptm. Liensberger, Oblt. Braun (special duties officer), Oblt. Müntefering. The special duties officers were non-flying members of the Stab.

Bf 110s of 15 Staffel (L1+GL, L1+LL), both with lightly mottled pale blue fuselage sides. The lighter areas beneath the code letters suggest overpainting.

Bf 110s L1+XB (foreground) and L1+YB, the aircraft of the Kommandeur and adjutant respectively. The Gruppe's trucks are parked along the edge of the forest.

"Airfield concert" at the forest's edge at St. Marie. Some overpainting of code letters is also obvious on aircraft L1+XB (Hptm. Liensberger); also note the narrowed white surround of the fuselage Balkenkreuz.

Fw. Jecke on his L1+BK. The aircraft call letter (third letter) was repeated on the upper (visible here) and lower sides of the wingtips.

An aircraft of 15 Staffel, clearly identifiable by the Staffel code letter "L" (fourth letter from the left).

Overland drive by 15 Staffel. In the second photo, second from the right, is a laughing Fw. Warrelmann. On the far right of the first photo is Lt. Altendorf.

They were called the "two Obergefreiters" of 15 Staffel (letter from Arndt to the author in 1996). Left Obgefr. Arndt, right Obgefr. Giglhuber on the beach at Dunkirk.

Adjutant (later Kapitän of 14 Staffel) Oblt. Zobel with his radio operator Uffz. Pellnat, photographed just before a mission.

Officers of 13 Staffel. From the left: Lt. Gorisch (killed 15/09/40), Lt. Beck (killed 13/08/40), Oblt. Glienke (killed 25/08/40), Staffelkapitän Oblt. Müller (killed 15/09/40).

Bf 110s of 13 Staffel (L1+GH in the foreground) parked randomly at the dispersal.

Oblt. Zobel seen climbing into the cockpit of his L1+YB assisted by two members of the ground crew. A white propeller spinner tip identified an aircraft as belonging to 13 Staffel, red 14 Staffel and yellow 15 Staffel.

Bf 110s of 15 Staffel (L1+DL, HL, FL, LL). The first two aircraft have pale fuselage sides, the others dark.

Second from the left is Hptm. Liensberger. Partially concealed behind him, identifiable by his blonde hair, is Oblt. Glienke. The others are, from the left, Oblt. Haarmann (special duties officer), medical officer, Oblt. Braun (special duties officer), medical officer.

Lt. Hessel and Lt. Eisele of 15 Staffel. Neither survived the war.

Right: Fw. Jentzsch of 13 Staffel. This front view illustrates well the relatively wide mainwheel tires used on the Bf 110.

On the reverse of the original photo is written: "Trouble brewing." Perhaps it has something to do with the captured French vehicles depicted in the photograph. Until June 1940 V/LG 1 was subordinate to ZG 2 commanded by Obstlt. Vollbracht. Above left, from the left: Hptm. Simon, Oblt. Schaefer, Obstlt. Vollbracht (ZG 2), Hptm. Liensberger (V/LG 1). Above right, from the left: Oblt. Schaefer (ZG 2), Hptm. Liensberger (V/LG 1) and Obstlt. Vollbracht (ZG 2).

Adjusting the variable-pitch propeller blades. Note the Wolf's Head emblem of V/LG 1.

Radio operator Uffz. Seufert, who flew with Lt. Goetze of 13 Staffel in aircraft L1+GH. The position of the swastika emblem in the center of the tail is unusual, as it usually appeared toward the lower, forward edge of the fin.

A propaganda service war correspondent visits the Gruppe. To the left of him is Oblt. Müntefering, right Hptm. Liensberger.

Visit by Göring to V/LG 1's base.

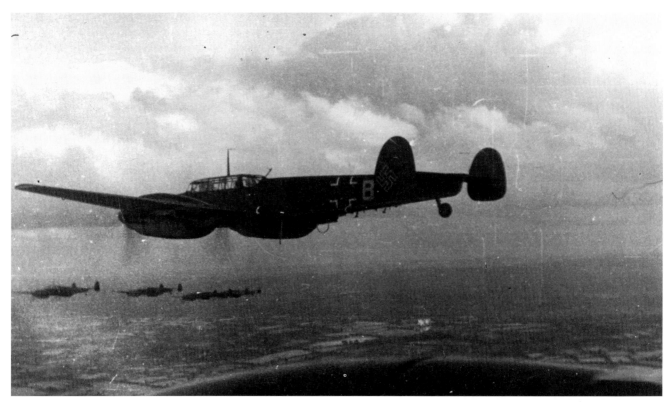

Formation flight by aircraft of 15 Staffel – three Ketten, each of three Bf 110s, photographed from the middle aircraft in the second Kette.

L1+OH of 13 Staffel receives an overhaul. Obfw. Kobert flew his last mission in this aircraft on 1 September 1940. It was not his machine; he wrote: "There was an old crow sitting on the field and I had to take it."

Obstlt. Grabmann, the Kommodore of ZG 76, next to the Kommandeur of V/ LG 1, Hptm. Liensberger. The two units flew joint missions during operations over England, including the last by V/LG 1 on 27/09/40.

Each day another crew had mess duty. Lt. Altendorf with radio operator Uffz. Arndt (below left), Uffz. Heldt with Obfw. Wagner (above) and Uffz. Schümichen with Obgefr. Giglhuber (below).

Lt. Becker of 14 Staffel. On 01/07/40 he was assigned to I/ZG 1, later to NJG 1, and was killed in action on 26/02/43 while serving with IV/NJG 1 (shot down by USAAF Mustangs during a daylight mission). In 1988 Eckart v. Bonin wrote: "Ludwig Becker was called the 'night fighter professor.' He shot down the enemy 'scientifically,' also achieved great success, received the Knight's Cross early, but then one day was himself shot down."

Staffelkapitän Oblt. Müller with his 13 Staffel. (above left) Müller, to the right of him Lt. Gorisch; (above right) Lt. Gorisch, Müller; (below left) from the left: Uffz. Seufert, foreground Lt. Gorisch, center background Oblt. Glienke, far right Oblt. Müller, in front of him Lt. Beck; (below right) officers, from the left: Oblt. Glienke, Lt. Gorisch, Lt. Beck, Oblt. Müller – all were killed in the fighting over England in 1940.

Conference between Staffelkapitän Oblt. Schnoor and the senior NCO of his 15 Staffel, Obfw. Tyrakowsky. Tyrakowsky survived the war but was killed soon afterwards in a tractor accident.

Base commander Obstlt. Voelker, Hptm. Liensberger, and Hptm. Mauke. The latter served for a short time as Kapitän of 14 Staffel, then fell ill and was sent home.

L1+GH of 13 Staffel behind the Wolf's Head standard of its predecessor Staffel.

Above: A rather dilapidated staff vehicle of V/LG 1 in Brussels. The later general and former Kommandeur of V/LG 1 Grabmann wrote in 1987: "This Mercedes is the staff vehicle that I was issued at the end of August 1939 at Barth in Pomerania with V(Z) LG 1. It was a privately-owned auto that was conscripted with mobilization." Left (with back to camera) is special duties officer Oblt. Haarmann, right the Kommandeur of V/LG 1, Hptm. Liensberger.

Right: Oblt. Fenske of 14 Staffel with orderly (on duty), was doctor in civilian life.

Oblt. Zobel in his L1+YB. Zobel was a member of 15 Staffel until May 1940; he then became adjutant and on 4 September 1940 Kapitän of 14 Staffel.

Handover of 14 Staffel to Oblt. Müntefering (former Technical Officer, member of the Stab) following the death of Staffelkapitän Oblt. Methfessel on 17 May 1940. From the left: Oblt. Zobel (adjutant), Oblt. Müntefering, Kommandeur Hptm. Liensberger.

Radio operator's view of his instruments. (Above) Day fighter: on the left side is the PG5 direction finder. In emergencies it was possible for the radio operator to climb over the step that separated the cockpits and assist the pilot by helping pull back on the control stick. This was made almost impossible in later models and in the night fighter version (below) by the installation of instruments on the step. Here the direction finder is seen on the right side of the cockpit. To the left of it are the low- (LF) and high-frequency (HF) receivers, while on the far left beside the top row of instruments is the radar scope for the various Lichtenstein systems.

Above the mounting for the aft-firing machine-gun of a Bf 110; below it are stowed the spare magazines.

Rest break; from the left: Oblt. Weckeiser, Oblt. Zobel, Hptm. Liensberger (on his pillow is the Tirolean eagle, the symbol of his home).

Right: Uffz. Busch, radio operator for Lt. Beck of 13 Staffel (until wounded on 08/08/40) wearing a "captured British tin hat." In the background is a Ju 52 transport aircraft.

Special duties officer Haarmann and Hptm. Liensberger in Brussels.

Special duties officer Oblt. Braun appears to be enjoying his ride in a captured British motorcycle. In the background is a tarpaulin-draped Bf 108.

Bf 110s of 15/LG 1 above the clouds.

L1+XB, the aircraft of the Kommandeur, being serviced. The same light finish as on the fuselage-sides is visible on the underside of the nose and engine cowling instead of the usual pale blue.

*Uffz. Arndt, radio operator for **Lt.** Altendorf of 15 Staffel, reads in the shadow of L1\HL of 13 Staffel.*

Oblt. Schnoor of 15 Staffel, considering which of the two dishes is preferable, or perhaps whether to have both together?

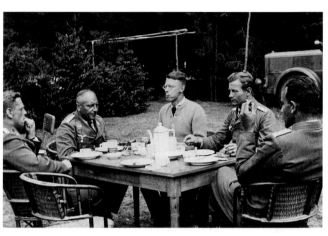

Members of the Stab at breakfast. From the left: special duties officer Oblt. Haarmann, special duties officer Oblt. Braun, medical officer Dr. Heinze, Oblt. Fenske and Hptm. Liensberger.

Fw. Datz of 13 Staffel.

Uffz. Pellnat, Oblt. Zobel's radio operator.

Members of the technical personnel at work. Clearly visible on the underside of the forward fuselage are the two muzzle openings for the twin cannon (20-mm Oerlikon MG-FF).

L1+AK. On 31 August 1940 the crew of Fw. Fritz and radio operator Obgefr. Döpfer of 14 Staffel ditched this aircraft in the Channel following air combat. Both were rescued from the water by the British.

The slaughtering and grilling specialists of 15 Staffel.

Second from the left is Uffz. Brüggow, surrounded by the technical personnel of his 15 Staffel.

Lt. Eisele with his radio operator Uffz. Lochow of 15 Staffel.

A Rotte (pair) of aircraft of V/LG 1 photographed from the cockpit of another Bf 110.

L1+XB photographed by Oblt. Zobel from L1+YB.

A French poster: "We will win because we are the stronger. Volunteer for the armed forces." Someone wrote over it in hand: "What hard luck!" No comment is necessary.

L1+CK, the aircraft of Oblt. Junge, the Kapitän of 14 Staffel, and his radio operator Fw. Bremser. They were shot down in this aircraft on 4 September 1940 and both men were killed.

Lt. Eichhorn of 14 Staffel beside his aircraft.

Right: In front of the situation map, from left: special duties officer Oblt. Haarmann, special duties officer Oblt. Braun, Oblt. Fenske, medical officer Dr. Weischer.

Below: Oblt. Müntefering (Kapitän of 14 Staffel) studies the map; to the left of him are special duties officer Oblt. Haarmann, Oblt. Glienke and the Kapitän of his 13 Staffel Oblt. Müller.

Four Bf 110s of V/LG 1.

Members of 13 Staffel. On the left is Fw. Klever, to the right of him Fw. Datz and his radio operator Uffz. Lämmel. It appears that this crew has copied Napoleon's familiar safekeeping of the right hand.

Radio operator Uffz. Lämmel, a mechanic and Fw. Datz pose in front of aircraft L1+JH.

L1+HL and L1+FL, two aircraft of 15 Staffel. Obfw. Wagner and his radio operator Uffz. Heldt were shot down over the Channel in this machine on 13 August 1940; both sank with the aircraft. Uffz. Schumichen and Obgefr. Glglhuber were shot down in L1+FL on the same day; both were rescued from the Channel by a British fishing boat. Approximately three weeks later, on 4 September, the crew of Uffz. Neumann and Uffz. Speier were killed in another L1+FL, which suggests that the codes of lost aircraft were painted on other Bf 110s.

The quiet periods between missions were always used to carry out maintenance work.

The faces of these members of 13 Staffel (Fw. Datz, Fw. Jentzsch, Fw. Klever, 2nd row left Fw. Meinig) reveal what they think of such "missions."

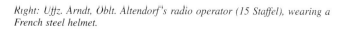

Over the British Channel Island of Jersey. On the right is visible the wingtip of a Bf 110 of 15/LG 1.

Right: Uffz. Arndt, Oblt. Altendorf's radio operator (15 Staffel), wearing a French steel helmet.

Mechanics of 13 Staffel at work – "There's no harm in a little fun!"

Fw. Datz of 13 Staffel poses in front of his machine with two members of the ground crew.

Fw. Klever of 13 Staffel before takeoff. Two more Bf 110s are visible in the background.

In the center Hptm. Liensberger, left Oblt. Müntefering, right Oblt. Zobel and Oblt. Müller.

Takeoff from the base at St. Marie. Photographed from the third aircraft, the first has taken off while the second taxies to position.

13 Staffel on parade before Staffelkapitän Oblt. Müller. From the left: Fw. Kobert, Fw. Klever, Fw. Jentzsch, Uffz. Dieckmann, Uffz. Busch; the rest are ground crew, with two French POWs on the extreme right.

L1+GL of 15 Staffel. Although Uffz. Bechthold was a member of 14 Staffel, he flew his last mission on 27 September 1940 in this aircraft. As a result, in English books Bechthold is described as belonging to 15 Staffel instead of 14 Staffel. While crews preferred to fly their own aircraft, damage or unserviceability sometimes meant that others had to be used instead. For example, according to Uffz. Bechthold's logbook, during the course of his 47 missions from May to September 1940 he flew Bf 110s with eight different codes, from both 14 and 15 Staffeln. In the case of Lt. Altendorf of 15 Staffel it was five.

Oblt. Weckeiser and Lt. Eisele of 15 Staffel. Eisele was killed, while Weckeiser was a POW in Canada until 1946.

Fw. Klever with two mechanics and his radio operator Uffz. Weller.

L1+AL and L1+BL of 15 Staffel, both with pale fuselage sides and narrowed white surrounds of the fuselage crosses.

Opposite below: Fw. Klever with radio operator Uffz. Weller of 13 Staffel in front of their Bf 110. Note that in this case the Staffel color has been applied to the spinner in the form of a narrow ring. In other photos the entire spinner is painted in the Staffel color (white for 13, red for 14, yellow for 15).

Uffz. Brüggow of 15 Staffel remembered: "French farmers stood at the side of the road selling strawberries. Almost every one of us took a crate and we ate on the spot until we really couldn't eat any more." In the middle row, third from the left, Lt. Altendorf, then Lt. Hessel and Fw. Warrelmann. Uffz. Brüggow is on the left next to Altendorf.

"Rocket takeoff" is written on the reverse of this photo. This is probably a reference to the dust and dirt stirred up by the aircraft during takeoff.

Preparations for a meal in front of 15 Staffel's mess tent. Note the spartan seating arrangements, consisting of bent branches.

Lt. Eisele of 15 Staffel after receiving the Iron Cross, Second Class.

Uffz. Pellnat, radio operator of Oblt. Zobel (adjutant, later Staffelführer of 14 Staffel).

France

Right: Oblt. Glienke of 13 Staffel and Hptm. Liensberger.

Two below: From the right: Hptm. von Boltenstern, Kapitän of 13 Staffel Oblt Müller, and Kommandeur Hptm. Liensberger. Von Boltenstern came to V/LG 1 from a bomber unit for retraining on the Bf 110. He then served for a short time as Kapitän of 14 Staffel and on 26 August 1940 was transferred to Erpr.Gr. 210 as Gruppenkommandeur. He was killed in action on 4 September, barely ten days later.

Six Bf 110s of 15 Staffel (L1+IL, BL and FL can be identified). Once again note the variety of camouflage schemes and different styles of fuselage cross.

Oblt. Fenske and Lt. Eichhorn of 14 Staffel inspect a Ju 87, presumably following a forced landing. The dive-bomber wears the code 6G+JR, which identifies it as belonging to III/StG 51 (later II/StG 1). The fourth (Staffel) letter "R" indicates the 7th Staffel of a Third Gruppe.

Left: V/LG 1 ground crew. Right: Lt. Eichhorn with his radio operator Uffz. Growe of 14 Staffel. On 31 August 1940 their aircraft was shot down over the Channel. Growe was fatally injured in air combat, but Eichhorn was rescued from the sea. He ended up in a POW camp in Canada, from where he returned in 1946.

Uffz. Bechthold of 14 Staffel in his aircraft L1+DK. He flew most of his missions in this aircraft from May 1940 until he was shot down on 27 September 1940 (27 of a total of 47 missions).

Lt. Altendorf of 15 Staffel.

Oblt. Schnoor and Hptm. Liensberger (right) supervise the loading of captured vehicles.

In the foreground L1+YB of adjutant Oblt. Zobel; in the background another Bf 110 is just lifting off.

Light anti aircraft gun positioned on the perimeter of V/LG 1's forward airfield.

Snack time for 15 Staffel. From the left: Fw. Reinhold, Uffz. Heldt, Uffz. Lochow, Uffz. Maresch and Uffz. Hamann.

Belly landing by Oblt. Schnoor of 15 Staffel in his L1+EL.

15 Staffel in front of the Eiffel Tower in Paris; from the left: Uffz. Dieckmann, 5th Fw. Meinig, 7th Lt. Schmidt, 8th Fw. Jentzsch, 10th Oblt. Glienke, Uffz. Busch, Oblt. Müller, 14th Lt. Gorisch, 16th Lt. Beck, Fw. Klever, Obfw. Kobert, Fw. Datz, Uffz. Seufert.

Aircraft of V/LG 1 over Paris (identifiable are L1+CL, AL, and KL of 15 Staffel).

Aircraft of V/LG 1 over Paris.

Nothing moves without fuel. No gasoline pump in sight, where does the hose lead? In the truck, from the right, Fw. Warrelmann, Lt. Hessel of 15 Staffel.

Shopping trip with Lt. Altendorf (15 Staffel).

Three members of 13 Staffel seen after receiving the Iron Cross, Second Class; from the left: Fw. Jentzsch, Uffz. Dieckmann and Fw. Klever.

Lt. Becker fiddles with the radio. To his left is Oblt. Müntefering, right Uffz. Harder. All were members of 14 Staffel.

Right: Title page from the magazine "Feuerreiter" (No. 25, Cologne, 15 June 1940); from the left Hptm. Liensberger, ordnance sergeant, adjutant Lt. Zobel, technical officer Oblt. Müntefering. The ring on Liensberger's finger came from the Austrian Military Academy; Liensberger was killed on 27 September 1940 and after the war the ring was returned to his parents from England.

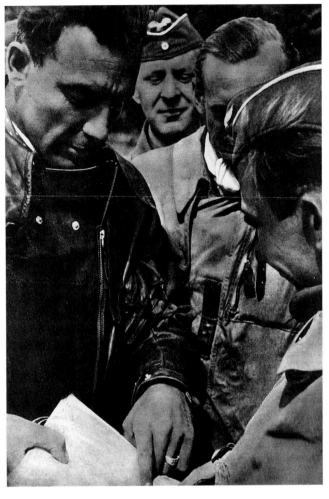

Below: Aligning the machine-guns of L1+AK of 14 Staffel. The aircraft was jacked up into a horizontal position and the guns were fired at a target positioned in front of it (not visible in this photo).

5

England

The *Gruppe* moved to Le Mans on 27 June. Personnel spent the night in private quarters. On the evening of the 29th the *Gruppe* moved on to Alencon, where it remained until its next transfer on 12 July. During this period the first ten missions over England were flown; the aircraft flew to Cherbourg, refueled and then began their missions.

4 July, 9:50 – 10:20 AM: Escort for Stukas into the Portland-Weymouth area, attack on convoy, anti-aircraft fire, no enemy aircraft encountered.

4 July, 3:15 – 4:25 PM: Escort for Stukas in attack on Channel convoy approximately 50 kilometers northwest of Cherbourg.

On 7 July the *Gruppe* escorted reconnaissance aircraft to Portland-Plymouth. This was repeated the next day, 8 July, with one mission in the morning and one in the afternoon. Two missions were flown on 9 July, once again escort for Stukas into the Plymouth area. Picket boats were attacked. This day saw the first combat with fighters of the RAF. The British consider this day the first of the "Battle of Britain."

The *Kapitän* of 13 *Staffel*, Oblt. Müller, did not take part in either mission and the Staffel was led by Oblt. Glienke. At about 9 PM, while over the Channel on the flight back, Obfw. Kobert noticed that the engines of Glienke's machine were not working properly and that the Bf 110 was steadily losing height. Attempts to establish radio contact were unsuccessful. While Fw. Datz and another four aircraft remained somewhat higher, Obfw. Kobert stayed with Glienke's Bf 110, which was obviously going to ditch in the sea. Maintaining a distance of about 100 meters, Kobert watched to see whether Glienke and his radio operator Uffz. Hoyer could get out of their machine. Glienke jettisoned the canopy shortly before touchdown, how-

ever the Bf 110 sank immediately. After a period of seconds which seemed like an eternity both men appeared, clearly visible in their yellow life vests. Fw. Meining, Obfw. Kobert's radio operator, immediately took a fix on their position and then Kobert set course for Cherbourg. Fw. Datz and the other four remained on station as long as their fuel situation permitted. At Cherbourg a He 59 of the sir-sea rescue service was alerted. As soon as Kobert had refueled he flew to the port to fly back to the crash site with the He 59. There was no time to lose as darkness was approaching. On the way to the crash site the other four machines were met heading for home, but the two men in the water were spotted immediately. The He 59 landed, took Glienke and Hoyer on board and brought them to Cherbourg. After refueling, at 9:40 PM Fw. Datz had also flown back to the crash site and returned at 10:20.

At noon on 11 July the *Gruppe* was supposed to escort Stukas to Weymouth Bay, however the mission was aborted on account of heavy cloud cover.

On the morning of 12 July the *Gruppe* moved to a base nearer the French Channel coast. The new forward airfield, which was to be the unit's home for the next six weeks, was located 10 kilometers south of Caen near Rocquancourt. The *Stab* established its command post in the Chateau Garcelles, while 13 and 14 *Staffeln* were quartered 3 kilometers east of Rocquancourt. 15 *Staffel* had its quarters in the Chateau Gouvix near Bretteville, 7 kilometers south of Roxquancourt. As well some men were billeted in private quarters. Most missions saw the fighters fly to Cherbourg to refuel before crossing the Channel; only a few were flown direct from Rocquancourt, such as on the afternoon of 12 July. That mission, armed reconnaissance off the Isle of Wight, resulted in attacks on freighters and combat with Spitfires.

The first mission on 13 July, escort for a Bf 110 reconnaissance aircraft to the Isle of Wight, had to be aborted on account of heavy cloud cover.

In the afternoon the *Gruppe* escorted a Do 17 reconnaissance aircraft to Portland. After a ten-minute battle with Spitfires, it appeared that the mission would end with no casualties. After reforming, a phase which could result in losses, the aircraft set course for home. However, Lt. Eisele and his radio operator Uffz. Lochow were still lagging somewhat behind the rest and they were promptly attacked from behind by several Spitfires. Their comrades warned them by radio but too late. The radio operators of 15 *Staffel* opened up on the attackers but with no effect. The range was too great, and the ideal line of position could not be reached. But the Spitfires broke away and disappeared. With both engines shot up, the Bf 110 went down in a glide. After about 500 meters the machine rolled onto its back, a possible sign that the crew were trying to bail out. The canopy roof was jettisoned and a figure could be seen. Then the incomprehensible happened. The parachute became hung up on the tail section and the figure was dragged down with it. The aircraft hit the water inverted and sank in a few seconds. Pieces of wreckage, part of a parachute and a life vest were subsequently seen floating in the Channel approximately 15 kilometers south of Portland.

Lt. Krebitz of 14 *Staffel* was more fortunate. He managed to nurse his heavily-damaged machine back to the French coast where he made a smooth landing, even though he was badly wounded. With a bullet lodged in his shoulder blade, a penetrating wound in one calf and another in one foot, he had lost two liters of blood.

Krebitz remained in hospital for a long time and as a result did not return to the *Gruppe*. On 12 November 1940 he was transferred to III/ZG 76 at Stavanger, Norway and a short time later to I/ZG 26 (3 *Staffel*). On 6 April 1941 (the first day of the operation against Yugoslavia) he took off from Szeged, Hungary to escort a formation of Stukas to Belgrade. He and his radio operator Uffz. Pack were shot down by Yugoslavian anti-aircraft fire near Subotika. Incidentally on the same day two more of the *Gruppe's* aircraft (2 *Staffel*) met a similar fate near Novi Sad.

His brother-in-law, Dr. Wolfgang Mayrhofer-Grüenbühl, retired minister president, wrote in 1993:

"In April 1941 Kurt Krebitz's mother received word that her son had been reported missing. She asked a clairvoyant if he was still alive. The latter said that her son had crashed but had been able to save himself. The clairvoyant was well known and had provided much accurate information. This news had a terrible effect: every time the bell rang the old woman was certain that it could only be her son. My wife, Kurt Krebitz's sister, wrote to me in every letter about the desperate waiting of her mother and of her steadily deteriorating nervous state. All that I could learn from the Luftwaffe command was that my brother-in-law was supposed to have crashed near Subotica. When I received a convalescent leave in 1942 I was given permission to travel to Subotica myself to make inquiries. In Topolya I met the German-speaking veterinarian Dr. Konrad, who told me that on 6 April 1941 a German aircraft had been shot down, fallen to earth in flames and that the crew had been killed. The aircraft had been flying very low and was hit by riflemen. No identity disks had been found. I demanded an exhumation and believe that I recognized my brother-in-law by his teeth. I informed my mother-in-law of the certain death of her son. In this way I was at least able to free her from the daily shock and the daily disappointment. The uncertainty had lasted more than a year. Dr. Konrad later sent me a picture of the gravestone."

Three missions on 14 July led to the area of the Isle of Wight. The *Gruppe* escorted reconnaissance aircraft which were supposed to investigate the British early warning system. At noon there was a joint attack with Stukas against a convoy and its escorting destroyer.

After a rest period from 15 to 20 July, on the 21st three missions were flown to the Isle of Wight. In the morning and afternoon the fighters provided escort for Stukas attacked convoys, while from 8 to 9 PM they rendezvoused with a group of Bf 110s and Ju 88s returning from attacks on the convoy and escorted them home. The job of attacking ships with Stukas was one of the most difficult for a Bf 110 *Zerstörer* pilot. It imposed a high work load on the pilot, as the low speed of the dive-bombers meant that the fighters had to weave constantly to stay with the formation. As well the targets were small, heavily armed and were protected by barrage balloons and defending fighters.

At approximately 5 PM 15 *Staffel* was heading for its base at Cherbourg. Far in front of Oblt. Weckeiser and Uffz. Brüggow hung a lone aircraft. When they drew nearer it turned out to be a Bf 110 of 14 *Staffel*. The two aircraft moved into formation and established radio contact. Uffz. Brüggow was very happy to hear the voice of his friend Uffz. Harder, who flew with Fw. Würgatsch. The two aircraft continued their homeward flight together after Harder had related that they had taken a considerable number of hits, including in the port engine. He also suspected that the undercarriage had been damaged. Oblt. Weckeiser recommended that they throttle back for a visual inspection of the undercarriage. He inched his Bf 110 toward the now lowered undercarriage. Caution was required, for wake turbulence could cause a potentially fatal collision. In spite of a close examination no visible damage could be seen. Nevertheless Oblt. Weckeiser recommended a wheels-up landing at Cherbourg. When it came time to land Würgatsch went first while Oblt. Weckeiser made a wide circle to the right and lined up behind him. After a smooth landing he taxied to the Staffel dispersal but it was empty. Weckeiser and Brüggow spotted a gathering at the side of the runway. Approximately 40 people were trying to raise a Bf 110 that was lying on its back. A doctor administered restorative injections to the two trapped men. But slowly, remorselessly, the heavy aircraft sank onto the bodies of the two men and crushed them to death. Many of those who had made the futile attempt to rescue the crew held back tears. It turned out that Fw. Würgatsch had tried a wheels-down landing after all, resulting in the machine flipping onto its back. Both men were buried in the cemetery in Cherbourg.

During an escort mission for reconnaissance aircraft to the Isle of Wight on 22 July British fighters attacked the formation. Lt. Goetze had one engine shot out but managed to reach home base on the remaining engine.

Two reconnaissance flights to the western tip of the Isle of Wight on 26 July met with no resistance from British fighters. From then until 8 August the *Gruppe* flew just one reconnaissance mission over the Channel, on 4 August.

From the British perspective, the heaviest attack on a convoy during the entire "Battle of Britain" took place on 8 August. Only four of twenty vessels reached their destination port of Swanage, west of the Isle of Wight. In the morning V/LG 1 escorted a Stuka unit attacking the convoy; no fighter opposition was met. However, the two subsequent missions at approximately 1:30 and 4 PM did result in combat with Hurricanes and Spitfires. Fw. Sturm and Fw. Brunner were shot down in flames and failed to get out before their aircraft crashed into the Channel. Uffz. Busch of 13 *Staffel*, Lt. Beck's radio operator, took a bullet through the thigh and was wounded in the eyes by splinters.

Hptm. Liensberger wrote in a letter home:

"Twenty tubs below in the water, so it begins. Our *Gruppe* had 16 aircraft in the air. The Stukas attacked the ships and we dashed about now above, now below. Suddenly all hell broke loose, they came in large numbers, 30 machines all at once. All around us brown aircraft and streaks of phosphorous. That was perhaps a dogfight."

The aircraft of Obfw. Jentzsch of 13 *Staffel* overturned on landing at Cherbourg. He suffered the same fate as Fw. Würgatsch on 21 July; like his friend he was buried in the cemetery in Cherbourg. Uffz. Dieckmann, Jentzsch's radio operator, was more fortunate. He was taken to hospital in Caen with serious injuries, some of which he had received in combat.

On 11 August the *Gruppe* escorted two *Geschwader* of Ju 88s in a major raid on Portland, then on the 12th a formation of bombers into the area south of the Isle of Wight. An attack by Spitfires was beaten off.

The 13th of August is famous as "*Adler Tag*" (Eagle Day). A large-scale operation had been planned for the first days of August but it was postponed several times on account of bad weather. With the forecast of favorable conditions it was scheduled for the 13th. As there was heavy cloud over the Channel again in the early morning, the attack was supposed to be postponed until the afternoon. However, not all units received the postponement order in time and some took off. V/LG 1 was already in the air at 6:30 AM, escorting bombers to Brighton-Guildford. KG 2, the unit being escorted, lost four Do 17s; the *Zerstörer* returned at about 8:30, having suffered no losses.

The main attack took place in the afternoon and was made in three waves. V/LG 1 flew in the first. The target area was Bournemouth-Portland-Isle of Wight. The bombers were suppose to attack airfields and radar stations. When the bombers crossed the Channel, at about 12:30 PM, the waiting Spitfires and Hurricanes were already visible as tiny dots in the sky, many tiny dots. Soon there was a wild dogfight in which the *Gruppe* lost five machines. All of the others returned with serious battle damage and wounded crew members.

In his book *Angriffshöhe 4000* published in 1964, Cajus Bekker wrote:

"The afternoon of Eagle Day began less than promisingly. The attack had been scheduled for 2 PM. But the weather had become even worse. A heavy fighter group, V/LG 1, was the first unit to take off from its base at Caen. There were 23 twin-engined Bf 110s. The *Kommandeur*, Hptm. Liensberger, was supposed to take his Gruppe to the south coast of England in the Portland area and conduct a fighter sweep there. Liensberger had just reached the British coast when he heard a warning call from one of his trailing machines: 'Spitfires from behind!' This call electrified the German crews. Liensberger therefore immediately ordered the formation of a defensive circle. Finally the defensive circle was closed. Two machines had been lost so far. When Liensberger's *Zerstörer* group finally returned from this difficult mission, five machines were missing with their crews, others counted dozens of bullet holes. This mission had a postscript two days later: 'And then there is the case of the *Zerstörer* group sent out on its own,' said Göring. 'How often have I already issued verbal and written orders that the *Zerstörer* units are only to be committed when necessary for reasons of range.' But Hptm. Liensberger's *Zerstörer* group had flown over to England completely on its own."

Grabmann (then a *Major* and *Kommodore* of ZG 76) wrote of this in 1989:

"The *'Zerstörer* group sent on its own' is a mystery to me. The story is completely unknown to me. V/LG 1 belonged to ZG 76 at that time. All of the *Zerstörer-geschwader* had specific, agreed-upon rendezvous points with the different bomber *Geschwader* depending on whether they were equipped with the He 111, Do 17 or Ju 88. The idea of V/LG 1 being ordered to 'free chase' is out of the question. It could only be that during its mission it missed its assigned bomber unit and subsequently went free chasing in an effort to find the bombers. As the destroyers were responsible for close fighter escort, on 13 August absolutely no *Zerstörergruppe* could be spared for other use. I am also unaware of any directive from Göring restricting the employment of the Bf 110 destroyers."

Hptm. Liensberger (Kdr. Of V/LG 1) wrote on two military post cards (dated 13/08/40):

"In the midst of feverish activity between two missions. It is so hectic over there that one scarcely has time to observe the effect of one's fire, another one is already there. They are pluck chaps, some of them 'great stunt pilots.' We are going over there again in two hours, things will turn out all right. – Today was a hard day for us, but we did it. Our *Gruppe* was alone over there. They were afraid that none of us might return, but we don't make it so easy for them, even though we lost machines."

The Bf 110 of Fw. Datz and radio operator Uffz. Lämmel caught fire after being hit. Wounded in the leg, Lämmel was unable to bail out under his own strength. Datz executed a half-roll and Lämmel was ejected from the machine. Datz sustained burns to his face. He floated in the Channel for several hours before the British fished him out of the water. Since he had suffered injuries to his corneas, for some weeks there was a danger that he had lost his eyesight. Datz was held as a prisoner of war in Canada until 1946. In August 1973 he was killed in the crash of a sporting aircraft. Lämmel's body washed ashore near Portland and he was buried in the naval cemetery there, where he still rests today.

The crew of Lt. Beck and Uffz. Hoyer, also of 13 *Staffel*, went down with their Bf 110 into the Channel near Bornemouth. Hoyer had only been flying with Beck for four days, after Uffz. Busch was wounded and put out of action on 8 August. The crew of Lt. Werner and Gefr. Klemm of 14 *Staffel* met the same fate as Beck and Hoyer.

The fourth and fifth losses affected 15 *Staffel*. Uffz. Brüggow witnessed the downing of Obfw. Wagner and Uffz. Heldt:

"Their aircraft dove straight toward the water at high speed. I was desperate, because there was no sign of movement from either man in the machine. I radioed: Paul bail out, jettison the canopy roof and bail out! I wiped away a few tears. I had to tear myself away from what was happening if I was to survive. Furiously I fired at everything that showed itself behind our machine, near or far, or tried to position itself there."

The second crew from this *Staffel* shot down had more luck. The Bf 110 of Uffz. Schümichen and Obgefr. Giglhuber was hit and set afire over Lulworth and crashed on Swalland Farm in Kimmeridge. Schümichen and Giglhuber were able to bail out. An excavation of the crash site in 1960 yielded some aircraft wreckage.

Schümichen described his experience:

"Our 15 *Staffel* was flying a defensive circle at an altitude of 7,200 meters. 14 and 13 *Staffeln* were 300 and 600 meters lower respectively. While we circled round and round, the British fighters placed themselves in a favorable, meaning higher, attack position while remaining at a safe distance well outside our defensive circle, in order to dive into the individual circles from above at maximum speed and then dive away. After about six circuits in the circle I suddenly heard my radio operator cry out and at the same instant took hits in the port engine and the instrument panel. The engine dropped from 1,800 to 1,000 RPM. Immediately after the attack, which was made by three fighters, I applied left rudder and got out of the stream of bullets. I got the machine up to 400 kph in a gentle dive, leaving a trail of smoke behind us. Seconds later there was a loud bang behind me in the area of the radio operator as fire broke out. Giglhuber had to bail out. It was more difficult for me to abandon the aircraft, for with the radio operator, rear canopy and machine-gun gone it pitched nose down and in no time the speed climbed to more than 500 kph. With my seat parachute I was pressed firmly between the upper edge of the seat and the roof of the canopy. After a great deal of effort I got both of my legs into the slipstream and was flipped over and thrown clear, losing one fur-lined boot and sock in the process. I let myself fall for several seconds, counting from one to nine, and then pulled the ripcord. The shock of the parachute opening was so great that I lost consciousness. At about 2,000 meters I was wakened by loud engine noise, a British fighter circled me and its pilot waved. Hanging in my parachute, the sea wind blew me several kilometers out over the Channel. I saw Giglhuber come down in the water before me, approximately four kilometers away. A British lobster fisherman had obviously watched my landing. He came over in his boat and pulled me out of the water. After I handed over my pistol, belt and parachute, he smiled and offered me a cigarette. We exchanged a few words while on our way to pick up Giglhuber. Then together we pulled my radio operator out of the water. When I climbed out of the boat I had difficulty walking on the stoney beach on my bare foot. A British soldier hurried over, took off his shoe and passed it to me. A short time later, when we arrived at a nearby coastal observation station, I received a friendly welcome from a uniformed man who had been treated well as a prisoner of war in Germany from 1916 to 1918. After a shower I was given a meal of fish with red wine and a pack of cigarettes."

Schümichen spent almost six years as a prisoner of war in Canada. His radio operator Giglhuber also remembered this last flight:

"On 13 August 1940 my pilot Schümichen and I were flying over the Isle of Wight at an altitude of more than 7,000 meters. We had taken off from Rocquancourt at approximately twelve noon with orders to escort a unit of bombers. While we were flying in a defensive circle, suddenly three Hurricanes came directly out of the sun. In the air battle that followed we received hits in the right engine and probably in a fuel tank, for while we were diving away there was a bang and then fire and smoke entered the cockpit. On orders from my pilot I jettisoned the cockpit hood and tried to bail out, which I was unable to do immediately on account of the high speed. While I was still struggling to get out there was another bang behind me and I was out. According to what my pilot Schümichen later told me, we were at an altitude of about 500 meters at that time. I probably struck the tail surfaces a glancing blow, for I had bruises on my left shoulder and for weeks could barely move my arm. I pulled the ripcord and my parachute opened immediately. I descended for about ten minutes, I would estimate five kilometers off the coast, into the Channel, from which I was pulled by a fisherman who already had my pilot Schümichen in his boat."

Giglhuber was kept a prisoner in England until 1941 and then in Canada. He was released in December 1946.

Radio operator *Gefreiter* Haas, who flew with *Oberleutnant* Junge in 14 *Staffel*, was wounded in air combat and was taken to Caen hospital with bullet wounds. There one leg had to be amputated after he developed blood poisoning.

Uffz. Arndt, radio operator of Lt. Altendorf of 15 *Staffel*, reported:

"On 13 August we took off from the Caen-South airfield at 12:15 PM for England. We were outnumbered by the British fighters and therefore adopted a defensive circle once again. Suddenly a British machine attacked the Bf 110 in front of us. Lt. Altendorf turned to the right and fired at the enemy. The latter rolled over its right wing and dove away, with Altendorf right behind it. He fired everything he had. Apparently in the heat of the dogfight AI had not secured the ammunition drum for the cannon properly, for when we dove it flew upward. I felt a heavy blow on the back of my head and heard something hit the roof of the canopy. At first I thought we were being shot at, but there were no aircraft to be seen anywhere. As a result of our split-S we were at low altitude. Since we were alone we flew back in the direction of France. Only now did the consequences of the blow on my head set in, I fell asleep. Altendorf later told me that there was a British fighter behind us which would surely have shot us down had not two Bf 109s, probably of the 'Ace of Spades' *Geschwader* (JG 53 - author) luckily also been on the way back to France. After shooting down the British fighter they escorted us to the airfield. Had they seen me lying unconscious in the machine? After landing I was taken on a stretcher to quarters, where I awoke some time later just as the mail from home was being distributed."

Arndt survived the war but had almost incredible luck:

"On the afternoon of 17 August 1943 we received the order to take off. Actually we were a night-fighter unit, but on 17 August there were so many enemy incursions that the night-fighters were alerted too. The takeoff order came rather late in the afternoon. The American bombers were already on the way back and we had to head west. As the bombers had already dropped their loads they were light and flying at maximum power toward the Channel coast. We had a hard time catching the formations, which consisted of several gaggles. They were flying in close formation and their defense was very strong. My pilot Lt. Altendorf spotted a machine between two gaggles and was about to attack it. He never got to, however, for British fighters appeared to rendezvous with the bombers. We were near the coast flying toward the sun, then I saw dots flashing in the sun. I warned my pilot but he said that they were surely returning German fighters. When they were out of the sun I saw the rounded wingtips and I knew – Spitfires. I alerted Altendorf but it was already too late. We couldn't even get away any more, for they were flying very high. When they spotted us they went into a dive. One machine after the other peeled off and turned toward us. There were about 15 machines. The first opened fire, I shot back. That's all I know, for I was hit in the head and probably knocked senseless. The following information is not from me but is the statement given by an infantry Leutnant when he delivered me to the military hospital in Geneva: he said that he and his driver had witnessed the downing from their car. After the enemy opened fire our machine caught fire and went into a dive. A dot separated itself from the aircraft and then a parachute opened. It was my pilot Altendorf (he told me this later, after my return to the *Staffel*). Then several more pieces came away from our machine, which by then was quite low. One part was me, then my radio operator's kit and the twin-barreled machine-gun. The armor plate was completely shot up. Whether I subconsciously pulled the ripcord or whether I became hung up when I was thrown clear is still a mystery to me today, for the parachute pack was damaged. I also ask myself why my radio operator's kit and machine-gun were found lying near the crash site, a crater in a meadow. Mystery after mystery which I can not solve. I was transferred to a neurological hospital in Brussels from the hospital in Genf (on account of my head injury). Approximately four weeks later, on 6 September 1943, I was released with the condition: grounded indefinitely! I ignored this and was forced to bail out over Berlin on 3-4 October 1943. I continued flying until just before the end of the war, then I was assigned to the ground forces in the anti-tank role. When the war ended I was in Neustrelitz. I walked to Schwerin, escaped from American captivity, went to Vechta."

Fw. Jecke of 14 *Staffel* also returned with serious leg injuries and had to spend several weeks in the navy hospital in Cherbourg. Jecke was killed on 5 October 1942 near Gilly, Belgium while serving with 2/NJG 4.

The crew of Fw. Klever and Uffz. Weller succeeded in landing their badly damaged machine at their own forward airfield after the Messerschmitt had been shot up by enemy fighters. Both had grazing wounds on the head and neck and they were taken to hospital in Falaise. Weller's injuries proved to be so serious that he could not return to the *Gruppe* after he was released from medical care and instead he was transferred to a company in northern Germany engaged in the development of secret weapons. He was captured by the Americans there in 1945 and held as a POW for a short time.

Klever was later killed while flying night-fighters with III/NJG 6 on 9 April 1945, just weeks before the end of the war. His Bf 110 went down over Neuhausen near Tuttlingen after the other two crew members had bailed out. Obfw. Klever failed to get out of his cockpit. The crash site was near Singen, the home of his former radio operator Weller.

The 13th of August was the second most costly day of operations so far for V/LG 1. Five machines failed to return from England. Seven airmen were killed and three captured. Three more returned with serious injuries.

The final tally from "Eagle Day": of more than 400 bombers and 1,000 fighters and destroyers that were sent over England on that day (in many cases three sorties) 40 remained in England. British losses were 13 Hurricanes and Spitfires shot down and 18 force-landed with battle damage. Both sides considered the result a success. But the intended elimination of the British fighter bases had not succeeded, the quantity of bombs dropped was insufficient to put the airfields out of action for any length of time.

On the late afternoon of 15 August there was an air battle with British fighters during an escort mission into the Portland area; V/LG 1 suffered no losses.

Toward midday on 16 August the *Gruppe* took off to escort bombers to Portsmouth. A late-afternoon mission took the *Gruppe* into the area west of London.

On 24 August V/LG 1 again returned from an escort mission to the Isle of Wight without loss.

On the late afternoon of 25 August an attack was launched against targets in the Portland, Weymouth Bay area. Three *Gruppen* of KG 51 (Ju 88) attacked port facilities in Portland. In addition to V/LG 1, direct fighter support was provided by two *Gruppen* of ZG 2 and III/ZG 76. Indirect escort was provided by three *Gruppen* from JG 2 and JG 53 as well as III/JG 27. A powerful and organized defense was waiting for the attack force. V/LG 1 was able to withdraw after a brief air battle. It was a stroke of luck when British fighters were not encountered until after the bombs had been dropped or on the way home as on this day. Nevertheless the crew of Uffz. Hamann and Uffz. Maresch of 15 *Staffel* was lost. As in most losses, no one saw exactly what had happened. It was merely observed on the fringe of events, out of the corner of the eye so to speak, that an aircraft veered off and left the formation or defensive circle. Help was only possible if the enemy was spotted behind the threatened aircraft and if the gunners were not engaged in defending their own machines. But what happened beyond the aircraft's horizon was the sole affair of the crew in question.

Oblt. Glienke and his radio operator Uffz. Stuck suffered the same fate. Both machines crashed into the Channel. Glienke had twice survived the loss of his Bf 110, on 4 January and 9 July, but this time he did not come back.

The aircraft of Fw. Röhring and Obgefr. Große of 14 *Staffel* was hit: Große reported:

"Our bombers were supposed to attack the tank farms in the Portland area. Fighter units, including our *Gruppe* V/LG 1, were assigned as fighter escort. As soon as we reached the English coast we came under heavy anti-aircraft fire and the first British fighters, Hurricanes and Spitfires, tried to intercept the bomber formations. We flew a closed defensive circle above the bombers and tried to keep the British fighters away from the bombers. As this air battle was very turbulent, I cannot say for certain whether our machine took a flak hit or was hit by an enemy fighter. Fw. Röhring screamed: we're hit and have to break off the mission! One engine was out and we went down in a dive from 6,000 to 400 meters. We tried to reach the French coast. In the middle of the Channel I suddenly noticed a Spitfire behind us, closing rapidly. I opened fire at it with the rear machine-gun. Then the fighter positioned itself beside us, as in a practice formation flight, wingtip to wingtip with about 10 to 20 meters between us. The pilot saluted with a friendly wave of his hand. We thought he had no ammunition left and wanted to escort us to the French coast. But suddenly he applied rudder and let us fly through a burst from his 8 machine-guns. I felt a heavy blow on my head, a bullet had torn off the right earphone from my helmet and a piece of my ear lobe. Fw. Röhrig was barely able to keep the now badly damaged aircraft in the air. Since we did not go down, the Spitfire moved in for a second attack, however God sent us a guardian angel, or better two, for two Bf 109s on their way home from England saw our desperate situation. They attacked the British fighter at the last moment and I believe shot it down. Thanks to the piloting skill of Fw. Röhring we reached the French coast and made a successful wheels-up landing near Cherbourg.

As a result of my wound I was unfit for duty for two months. Uffz. Jäckel joined Fw. Röhring as his radio operator. At the end of 1940 I became the radio operator of Lt. Leickhart, who had meanwhile returned to the *Gruppe*, since renamed I/NJG 3, after being wounded on 11 May.

I flew my 125th and last mission with Leickhart (who served with 14 *Staffel* in 1940) on 23 February 1944 with I/NJG 5. We had been transferred to this unit together in autumn 1942. At about 1 PM we and two other crews received the order to take off. A formation of approximately 30 Flying Fortresses had been reported entering the airspace over the north of Germany. We found the formation in the Greifswald area. Because of the heavy return fire we could not get close enough to use our 210-mm rocket

projectiles successfully and they missed the target. On the other hand all three of our machines were hit and had to make forced landings. I was badly wounded by an explosive shell and my left arm had to be amputated at the shoulder. After recovering I was transferred to the Luftwaffe High Command, 13th *Fliegerregiment*.

I was stationed at Berlin-Döberitz until May 1945, then during the last weeks of the war we were transferred to Rosenheim. I never reached the post in Rosenheim for while on my way there I got caught up in the Prague uprising and was captured by the Russians. On account of my wound I was released from the military camp at Neubisteritz at the end of July 1945."

On the late afternoon of 26 August the *Gruppe* flew escort for KG 55. Beginning at approximately 5 PM the Portsmouth area was raided on a front of 60 kilometers.

The first attack on London followed three days later on the 29th. It was a so-called "provocation action." A small number of bombers with a large number of Bf 109s and Bf 110s were supposed to simulate an attack in order to draw the British fighters into the air where they could be engaged in combat.

Two missions were flown on 30 August. At noon the target was Croydon airfield near London, at 4 PM facilities in the Thames Estuary.

The next day, 31 August, saw V/LG 1 suffer further casualties when two aircraft were shot down. Its mission was: "Direct escort for the attack on Cambridge airfield and the Rolls-Royce aircraft factory located near this city." Strong British fighter units intercepted the German aircraft just north of London. Hurricanes attacked the destroyers, which were flying in a defensive circle.

Both aircraft lost belonged to 14 *Staffel* and were crewed by Lt. Eichhorn/Uffz. Growe and Fw. Fritz/Obgefr. Döpfer. The following is Döpfer's account:

"The Hurricanes' attack caught us completely by surprise. I can only remember that a Hurricane suddenly came out of the sun and fired. All I could do was warn my pilot: attack from behind! I myself opened fire at the attacker, whereupon he veered away. I am certain that I hit him. My pilot swung our Bf 110 away to the left, but at that moment we were attacked by another Hurricane and I heard bullets striking our machine. As a result of this combat we had become separated from our unit and had also lost a great deal of height. I heard my pilot curse: the port engine is burning! I am putting her into a dive – perhaps the fire will go out. Prepare to bail out! – I pulled the emergency lever to jettison the canopy roof, but it failed to work, apparently it had been damaged by gunfire. The port engine was still burning and the starboard one was now sputtering too. We were still over land. My pilot called to me: I am trying to reach the Channel, try to jettison your canopy roof. Thank God, it suddenly flew away, soon afterwards our Bf 110 touched down on the water. Our machine sank quickly and we were unable to free our dinghy. We had been in the water for about an hour when a fishing boat came chugging towards us. The crew worked for more than ten minutes to pull us onto the deck with ropes. When they finally succeeded we were given dry clothes. The really necessary warming took place in the engine room and the captain brought us a glass of whisky. We thought it was water and drank it down in one swallow."

Döpfer returned from prisoner of war camp in Canada in 1946 as did Fritz.

Eichhorn, the survivor from the other machine, wrote of his experience on that day:

"We took off early that morning with orders to escort a bomber unit in an attack on the Rolls-Royce aircraft factory near Cambridge. Near Bishop's Stortford, halfway between London and Cambridge, my element, which was flying at the rear of the Staffel, was attacked from behind by Hurricanes. I was element leader, my wingman was Fw. Fritz with his radio operator Obgefr. Döpfer. The attack by the Hurricanes came as a complete surprise, and the only thing I noticed was bullets striking my canopy and the whole aircraft. The right engine immediately caught fire. My radio operator, Uffz. Growe, fired and cried out simultaneously. In order to get away from our attackers I dove from our altitude of 6,000 meters to sea level. There was fog there and no one followed me. I now realized that my radio operator had been hit and was lying dead in his cockpit. With just one engine running I was now flying along a few meters above the surface of the water. After about ten minutes the remaining good engine lost power and I was forced to ditch. First, however, I jettisoned the completely shattered upper part of my canopy and got my dinghy out of the aircraft. After the Bf 110 touched down on the water it sank very quickly and I had difficulty getting out in time. In the water I made several attempts to get into the life raft, but my heavy, water-soaked flying boots made this very difficult. Finally I was in the raft. After two hours I was picked up by a fishing boat and put ashore near Margate at the end of the Thames Estuary. I remained a prisoner of war in Canada until 1946."

Lt. Eichhorn and Fw. Fritz had been shot down by Hurricanes of 601 Squadron. The squadron's daily report contains the following remarks concerning the shooting down of Lt. Eichhorn:

"Yellow 1 attacked a Me 110, which was just being attacked by another Hurricane. It went down about 5,000 feet in a dive. Yellow 1 had the height advantage and was able to overtake the Me 110 with full power. He opened fire from 250 feet, the starboard engine was hit immediately and glycol spurted out. The rear gunner was silenced. The Me 110 went down in a steep dive to the sea, but Yellow 1 succeeded in overtaking it again and attacked again while in the dive. He fired at the port engine, from which came white and black smoke. The starboard engine then stopped and the Me 110 was only a few feet above the surface of the sea. Yellow 1 reported that he clearly heard repeated calls for help in German and heard the position being relayed. Apparently he was on the same frequency as 601 Squadron. Yellow 1 was forced to break away as he had expended his ammunition."

V/LG 1 flew with II/JG 26 and III/KG 76 on 1 September in a raid on an airfield in the London-Thames Estuary area. 13 *Staffel* lost one aircraft en route to the target. The pilot, Obfw. Kobert, described what happened:

"When it came time to take off at about 2 PM one of my machine's engines was not working properly. A reserve machine, an old crow, sat on the airfield perimeter and I took it. I and my *Schwarm*, which included Lt. Goetze and Lt. Schmidt, were at about 5,000 meters, halfway between the Channel and London. As on most missions over England my *Schwarm* flew top cover approximately 800 to 1,000 meters above the *Gruppe*. In the event of attack I would dive beneath the others and be protected by them. My right engine kept losing power. The several Hurricanes attacked from above and behind. They opened fire from long range, something that usually never happened. I was about to peel off into my *Gruppe* when a Hurricane hit one of my engines, which immediately began to smoke. I had to shut down the engine. As a result of this incident and my reduced speed I was unable to join up with the *Staffel* and I lost sight of the *Gruppe*. The other members of my *Schwarm* were also gone, I was alone. But I could also not see any more Hurricanes. At 5,000 meters in a brilliant blue sky, I wanted to sneak home furtively on one engine. But on the way two Hurricanes got me again. I repeatedly tried to dive and then climb into firing position, but with one engine I soon lost a great deal of altitude in this mess. Now the left engine also began to falter, overtaxed by continuous flying at full power, until it finally quit altogether at about 200 meters above the ground. The intercom was out, so I did not know what was happening to my gunner, Fw. Meinig. I selected a small meadow for the now necessary forced landing, which was very difficult on account of the many hedges and fences. Then I nosed the machine into a wire fence to reduce speed. I did not have too much room, as there were large trees at the end of the field. The landing came off quite well. I had previously jettisoned the canopy roof so that I was free. I immediately jumped out, my radio operator was also scrambling clear and I gave him a hand.

We were quite near a village and after about five minutes two policemen came. Several farmers also rushed to the scene, rather irritated as I had hit some sheep while landing. The police kept them away and soon brought us to the police station. I never took my pistol with me to England, what good would it have been anyway.

I was immediately separated from Meinig and I did not see him again until weeks later in Oldham camp. At the police station one of the policemen laid his pistol on the desk and made a telephone call, repeatedly picking up his pistol and pointing it at me. Then a woman arrived. I later learned that her sister was married to a university professor in Heidelberg. She could speak some German and I had my school English. She convinced the policeman that I was harmless, whereupon he put away his pistol. I traded my R6 cigarettes to the woman for some English ones, she was also otherwise very friendly and invited me to tea. I was unable to accept, however, as a military truck from the nearest base picked me up and took me to an army post. There I was placed in a cell with a wooden plank-bed, but bright military bedclothes. I spent fourteen days in the Hyde Park interrogation camp, where they came for me at all hours of the day and night. From Oldham camp in 1941 I went to Canada, from where I returned in 1946."

Pilot Officer English of 85 Squadron, who participated in the shooting down of Obfw. Kobert, wrote in his combat report:

"I spotted a formation of Dorniers which were approaching the south end of London, so I flew toward them to intercept. Pilot Officer Lewis joined me and we positioned ourselves to attack from in front. I attacked the last Do 17, but when I turned right from below several Me 110s attacked me from above. I broke away and came back, but my attack was hindered by two Me 110s which attacked me from above and behind. I could only fire one short burst. I dove to safety in a thin layer of cloud and stayed there until I thought the Me 110s had returned to their defensive circle. When I came out of the clouds I saw a lone Me 110 west of the main formation heading south. I attacked from the right and hit the starboard engine, which stopped. I made the next attack from the left, from the blind spot. By the time I had closed to within ten yards of the Me 110 my ammunition was gone. During my first attack I fired a burst of 5 seconds, during the second one of 7 seconds. I broke away to the right and the Me 110 rolled almost onto its back and went down in a dive. I followed it and it flew away at approximately 4,500 feet and continued to descend. Finally it made a belly landing in a field after it had broken through a fence. It was south of the canal that runs between Harn Street and Hythe, halfway between Ashford and Lydd. The two members of the crew climbed out of the aircraft. After my first attack it appeared that the Me 110 could maintain altitude and was trying to reach France even though only one engine was running. The Me 110s appeared to fly closer to the bombers than usual. It was very difficult to attack the bombers before the Me 110s came down."

Together with the *Staffelkapitän* Oblt. Müller, Obfw. Stegemann and Obfw. Schob, Obfw. Kobert was one of 13 *Staffel's* most experienced pilots. He had been present since the *Gruppe's* formation in 1937 and was the first to have his blind-flying endorsement. Schob was transferred to ZG 76 in March 1940 and he survived the war. Stegemenn was killed in action on 21 May 1940, while Müller died on 15 September, fourteen days after Kobert's belly landing.

Kobert does not subscribe to the commonly held view that the Bf 110 was generally inferior to the Spitfire and Hurricane:

"I would not say that the British fighters were superior to the Bf 110. Each possessed certain advantages and disadvantages. Under equal conditions much depended on the pilots. But I would like to make one thing clear: the nature of our missions placed us at a grave disadvantage compared to the British. The fighter pilot's motto has always been: see and attack at once! But on our missions this applied only to the British. They could initiate their attacks from a safe altitude, where and when they wanted. On the other hand we as direct escorts were tied to our slower-flying bombers. We had to wait until the British attacked, usually in superior numbers. In order for us to have at least some measure of mutual protection in this disadvantageous situation we formed one or two vertically staggered defensive circles."

(On this topic: A comment from Grabmann from 1989: "Concerning the performance of the Bf 110: I myself carried out very many comparison flights with the Bf 109, Bf 110 C against Bf 109 E. Speed equal, Bf 109 somewhat better in a climb, Bf 110 somewhat faster in a shallow dive. Dogfighting: 50:50. It was the same against the Spitfire. It was a different picture with the night-fighter Bf 110 because of the extra equipment required for night fighting.")

During the return flight on that 1 September 15 *Staffel* lost the crew of Fw. Jäckel and Flg. Rösler. The pair had joined the *Gruppe* from Replacement Training *Staffel* (*Ergänzungsstaffel*) 1 at Vaerlöse-Copenhagen several days earlier. For unknown reasons the machine went down south of London near Brasted and exploded on impact. For this reason the crew could not be identified. The cross on the grave in the nearby St. Martin cemetery bore the inscription: "Two unknown German airmen." Jäckel and Rösler were reburied in Cannock Chase military cemetery as part of the general reinternment of German fallen.

On the afternoon of 2 September V/LG 1 flew escort for a unit of Do 17s. The intended target was an airfield east of London. The fighters engaged the enemy but returned without loss.

The next mission came two days later, on 4 September. The target was the Vickers-Armstrong factory near Weybridge. The *Gruppe* was assigned to protect *Erprobungsgruppe* 210, a trials unit equipped with bomb-carrying Bf 110s, while it made its attack. While en route to the target Erpr.Gr. 210 lost an aircraft at 2 PM even before it reached the English coast. It was the unit's only casualty on this day. *Kommandeur* Hptm. von Boltenstern and his radio operator Fw. Schneider crashed into the Channel. The circumstances of the loss are not known; the official casualty report states: "Missing after being fired on by enemy fighters; declared dead on 10/03/44." Von Boltenstern went down with the aircraft, while Schneider's body later washed ashore near Newhaven. In mid-August von Boltenstern had been *Kapitän* of 14 *Staffel* of V/LG 1; Schneider flew with him as he had with the previous *Staffelkapitän*.

The formation reached Weybridge and in the factory the alarm was sounded only minutes before the attack came. As a result heavy damage was done to the installation and production was halted for several days. The *Gruppe* circled overhead until the Bf 110 bombers left the target area. At this point British fighters showed up and shot down three aircraft of 14 *Staffel*.

The Bf 110 of Fw. Röhring and Uffz. Jäckel crashed onto Waterloo Farm near West Horsely. Röhring was buried in the Brookwood military cemetery and his gravestone still stands there today. Pieces of the wreck excavated in 1977 are now on display in the London Air Museum.

Jäckel, who was able to parachute to safety, remembered his last flight:

"The 4th of September was a cloudless autumn day. We sat or lay beside our machines. Out in the fields the French were harvesting grain. The farmers loaded the wagons, women and girls helped, a peaceful world. Then the telephone rang, the *Staffelkapitän* was summoned to a mission briefing by the *Gruppenkommandeur*. When he returned everyone had to gather round and he informed us of our mission. We flew across the Channel in a cloudless sky and reached our target, the Vickers aircraft factory near Weybridge. The escort fighter *Schwarm* soon disintegrated into individual combats with Hurricanes and Spitfires. Then the British fighters disappeared and the *Staffel* assembled. There were four machines. Our *Staffelkapitän*, *Oberleutnant* Junge, made one more wide circle and then we set course for the Channel and France. Suddenly I saw four fine lines behind us: four British fighters. I immediately informed *Feldwebel* Röhring and heard the other radio operators calling out the fighters. Oblt. Röhring turned into the fighters but they were already upon us. I fired, then I saw the blue muzzle flashes and we were hit. I felt a blow on my left shin. When I looked around Fw. Röhring was slumped to the side and flames were coming out from under his seat. Get out! I screamed and pulled the red jettison lever. The canopy flew away and I was yanked out. I lost consciousness. When I woke up I saw blue sky above me but heard no engine noise. I felt the wind blowing past me to the left and right, my arms swung in the air. Then something struck me: you have bailed out! I immediately pulled the ripcord. The chute opened with a rustle, the harness squeezed me, and I had the feeling that I was traveling upward. Then I was dangling beneath my parachute, the wind had pulled off my flying boots. Blood was dripping from my left leg. I wanted to go to sleep, nevertheless I had to stay awake, my head repeatedly fell forward. In the distance I saw the French coast as a line. Much air rushed through the small hole above in the parachute and England, with its square, fenced meadows, came ever nearer. Once a British fighter came and circled me several times. I landed in a field. Soon several civilians arrived carrying shotguns. One cursed, one tried to console me. Then I saw a crowd of people behind me, led by a young blonde girl in a summer dress. That revived my spirits somewhat. Two soldiers came and carried me through the cordon of people, who held out packs of cigarettes, to a police station where I was given first-aid."

Jäckel returned from captivity, most of which was spent in Canada, in 1946.

The aircraft of Oblt. Junge and Uffz. Bremser crashed near Dorking and burned out. Both airmen are buried in the

Brockwood military cemetery. Excavations of the crash site in 1978 produced several pieces of wreckage.

The third Bf 110, crewed by Lt. Braukmeier and Obgefr. Krischewski, crashed into the Channel. Both men were reported missing and declared dead in January 1942.

The fourth loss affected 15 *Staffel*. The crew of Uffz. Neumann and Uffz. Speier, which had been transferred to the *Gruppe* from the *Zerstörer* Replacement Training *Staffel* in Copenhagen only fourteen days earlier, almost managed to make it to the French coast in their badly shot-up machine, however two weeks later Speier's body was washed ashore near Berck sur Mer and two days later Neumann was found on the beach at Boulogne. Today both men rest in the German military cemetery in Bourdon.

Uffz. Pfaffelhuber's radio operator Uffz. Banser, who had sustained serious bullet wounds in combat, was taken to hospital in Caen. His place was taken by Uffz. Kramp, who had flown with Fw. Warrelmann until 11 August. On that day Warrelmann broke a collarbone in a motorcycle accident on a Harley-Davidson.

The *Gruppe* had lost 17 machines within the last month, approximately 60% of its authorized strength. 24 crewmembers had been killed, 9 wounded and 9 were POWs in England. Deliveries of replacement aircraft and personnel were sluggish and in September only one replacement crew, Lt. von Bonin and Uffz. Johrden, was received. The missions became increasingly difficulty, and consequently losses increased. The first enemy fighters were now being met over the Channel en route to the target. And the second line of fighters waited over the broad fields near Hastings, and if this was penetrated there awaited the witch's cauldron of metropolitan London. An efficient early warning system guided the British fighters to their opponents. The Bf 110s formed a solid block, called a spiral, defensive but also panic circle, which turned over the bombers to be protected. Flying even higher, Bf 109s provided the indirect escort. If one survived the flight to the target there was still the reversal and the equally dangerous flight home. If one did escape from the cauldron it was not for long, for the patrol lines at the coast and the center of the Channel had to be crossed as well. In many cases extreme low-level flight was the only salvation. It was also the undoing of many whose aircraft had been shot up in combat resulting in the loss of an engine.

On the morning of 6 September V/LG 1 flew its eighth mission into the London area since the start of these operations on 29 August. The heaviest attack so far took place on 7 September, when the *Gruppe* provided escort for Do 17s of KG 76. On 8 September V/LG 1 was called upon to escort a formation of He 111 bombers, again into the London area.

The crew of Uffz. Pfaffelhuber and Uffz. Kramp failed to return from the next mission, one day later on 9 September.

Directly over London there was a dogfight with Hurricanes of 310 Squadron. Pilots of this squadron wrote in their combat reports:

"An Me 110 was seen to break formation with smoke coming from one engine, probably the result of a previous attack. It went down in a dive and it was seen to disappear into the haze. One pilot got behind eight Me 110s, which scattered. He chased one and attacked it three times, while the Me 110 tried to escape by climbing and diving. One motor was smoking. The pilot fired another burst at the Me 110 in the dive, whereupon the engine that was smoking began to burn. As his own machine was damaged and vibrating, the pilot broke off the engagement."

Another account:

"The pilot attacked an Me 110 which was on the tail of a Hurricane. He fired a long burst at the Me 110, while it pulled up to the right. The Me 110 now went into a steep dive, smoke pouring from both engines, and it appeared that it was on fire as the pilot saw a red glow."

These reports illustrate the difficulty in allocating claims by pilots for enemy aircraft shot down. As a result, on both sides victories were confirmed only after intense scrutiny, requiring the presence of a witness, and usually after the passage of a year.

The Bf 110 of Uffz. Pfaffelhuber and Uffz. Kramp crashed on the Maori sports field in New Malden and exploded on impact. Some pieces of the machine were dug up in the 1970s and were placed on display in the military aviation museum at Tangmere. Since 1963 the remains of the pilots have rested in the German military cemetery at Cannock Chase.

Alfred Stier, then an *Unteroffizier*, wrote in 1989:

"I always flew with pilot Alois Pfaffelhuber at the *Zerstörer* Replacement Training *Gruppe* at Schleißheim, then after our transfer to V/LG 1 the missions in France, until in August I was transferred back to the Reich. I still have a photo of Alois that I always carried with me. He was such an excellent comrade and good pilot. He was engaged and he passed his free time by placing a photo of his fiancee in front of himself and playing heart-rending gypsy melodies on his violin."

Horst Brüggow, another member of 15 *Staffel*:

"On 9 September our *Staffel* took off for London with just three aircraft, only two returned. Uffz. Pfaffelhuber and his radio operator Uffz. Kramp did not come back. They were shot up while in the defensive circle and came to grief on the flight back. It don't think it is necessary to say that the loss of these two left deep scars on we survivors. Alois Pfafflhuber gave us so many contemplative evening hours, when, with the day's missions over, he simply relaxed, pulled out his violin and skillfully and with feeling played away our inner worries. He did us a favor, but his thoughts and his playing was for his fiancee, far away at home. But Otto Kramp, one of the 'old Barth hands,' and I are linked by peacetime experiences so beautiful that I will probably never forget them. But we did not have much time to comprehend, to relax. That was probably also the reason why we had become so coarse, direct and brief with our words."

On 10 September 1940 the then *Leutnant* and later *General* Gordon Gollob wrote to Hptm. Liensberger (Gollob and Liensberger had flown together in the Austrian Air Force in 1934):

"Dear Horst! I could kick myself for not going along on this flight to see you. I knew that you were a *Kommandeur*, but I had no idea where in the world to find you. Never in my entire flying career have I been in such a shameful position as now. You will no doubt have heard. If you want to and can do something for me then send for me. Perhaps you will need a *Staffelkapitän* before it's over. I really don't know what I'm supposed to be doing here. I am not qualified in instrument flying, the precondition for night-fighters, and I am not going to be. As a result I am completely out of place here as chief. They're supposed to produce a blind flying expert here, but not me. It's enough to drive one to despair. If need be you can request me and justify it by saying that I can't fill my position here anyway. Under no circumstances do I want to remain with the night-fighters. If nothing else happens I will just have to write a request, or I can write a request if the front becomes short of men. So please think of me and write to me if you can. All the best. Break a leg! Gollob."

Surely Gollob could not know that V/LG 1 would exist only a few days after the arrival of his letter, having been almost wiped out, and that Horst Liensberger would be among those killed.

On 11 September the *Gruppe* received orders to escort Bf 110 bombers of *Erprobungsgruppe* 210 in an attack on the Spitfire factory near Southampton that afternoon. This time the fighters survived the ensuing air battle without loss.

In Great Britain the 15th of September is celebrated as

"Battle of Britain Day." Throughout the late morning and early afternoon of that day in 1940 large formations of German aircraft streamed toward the London area. They were met by 31 squadrons of the RAF with approximately 300 Spitfires and Hurricanes. The Luftwaffe suffered its heaviest losses since 15 August, more than 50 aircraft. The British lost 30 which crashed, while another 26 were damaged and made forced landings. V/LG 1 flew escort for Do 17s of II and III/KG 2. This formation withstood the persistent attacks by British fighters until the return flight, when three Do 17s and Bf 110s were shot down.

The first of V/LG 1 to be shot down was the *Kapitän* of 13 *Staffel*, Oblt. Müller. His machine went down near Hothfield, near Ashford, about 20 kilometers short of the Channel coast. Oblt. Müller and his radio operator Fw. Hoffmann both probably bailed out, or perhaps Müller made an unsuccessful attempt at a forced landing after his radio operator abandoned the aircraft. In any case Müller succumbed to his injuries in Hothfield hospital the same day, while Hoffmann died in Chartham military hospital approximately 20 kilometers to the north. Until their reburial in the Cannock Chase military cemetery in 1962 Müller rested in Charing cemetery while Hoffmann was buried in Chartham.

The crews of Lt. Gorisch and radio operator Uffz. Gerigk, also of 13 *Staffel*, and Lt. Adametz and Obgefr. Stief of 14 *Staffel* made it to the Channel but were then shot down. The sea became their grave. As only three Bf 110s altogether were lost on this day, the following combat report by 213 Squadron probably refers to the two last-mentioned aircraft:

Lt. Cottam dove vertically on a Do 17, damaged it, and after he had lost sight of it flew on to Dungeness, where he saw a Spitfire attacking a Bf 110. He joined up and helped shoot it down into the sea.

Sergeant Snowdon had not had an opportunity to attack a Do 17, so he too flew on to Dungeness to look for stragglers. And after he had spotted a Bf 110 he attacked it and shot it down. It crashed into the sea. The crew of this Bf 110 was seen in the water.

The Do 17 was often mistaken for the Bf 110, but in this case the type may have been correct, because there is no analogous Do 17 loss. Whether there really was a crew in the water is not known. All four airmen remained missing.

After a free chase mission in the London area on the morning of 16 September it appeared that V/LG 1 would be withdrawn from combat indefinitely on account of the heavy casualties it had suffered. Between 4 July, the date of the first mission over England, and 15 September the three *Staffeln*, each of which had an authorized strength of 9 aircraft, had lost 25 machines. In spite of the arrival of replacements, which lagged far behind losses, the *Gruppe* now had just 11 crews and many of its aircraft were in urgent need of repair or overhaul. V/LG 1 had practically ceased to exist. In September the weather deteriorated noticeably and the enforced pauses benefited the defenders more than the attackers, for they were in a better position to recognize developing systems moving from west to east. The ratio of forces continued to shift in favor of the British fighters, while German losses assumed even more alarming proportions.

During the period 21 to 26 September crews from the *Gruppe* flew to Mannheim to have urgently needed repair work carried out, or to Augsburg to collect new aircraft. Six Bf 110s landed at Rocquancourt on the 26th. The ferry crews subsequently brought a Ju 52 to the base near Ligescourt, from where two *Staffeln* of V/LG 1 had been flying their missions since 29 August (one *Staffel* had remained at Rocquancourt south of Caen). The uneasy feeling that the next day might see a return to the skies over England disappeared when the rumor surfaced that V/LG 1 was not going to be committed. That would have meant a chance to unwind, perhaps home leave with the family or fiancee. Hopes were raised.

Oblt. Zobel with his radio operator Uffz. Pellnat of 14 Staffel.

V/LG 1 was based at the airfield in Alencon from 29 June to 11 July 1940. 15 Staffel was billeted in this house.

Members of 15 Staffel in front of their quarters in Alencon, where they lived for 12 days. At the back officers Oblt. Weckeiser and Lt. Altendorf.

At the dinner table at Alencon. In the foreground is Lt. Altendorf, second from the left Fw. Warrelmann.

On the right a pensive-looking Obfw. Wagner with his radio operator Uffz. Heldt beneath their L1+KL. Perhaps Wagner had some inkling of the missions to come.

L1+XB, the aircraft of Hptm. Liensberger, on the airfield at Alencon. Note the "X" on the starboard wingtip as well as the overpainting of the factory code on the fuselage. Behind the Bf 110 is parked a Ju 88.

Left: Written on the reverse of this snapshot is: "Something must have been going on here!" Far left Hptm. Liensberger. Right: Uffz. Pellnat (left, radio operator of adjutant Oblt. Zobel) and Uffz. Köpge (radio operator of Hptm. Liensberger) in front of L1+XB. Note the color scheme applied to the spinner (2/3 white, 1/3 green). The letter "X" was in the same green with a white outline.

The tail of a Bf 110 of V/LG 1 over the French coast.

Photo taken by Oblt. Zobel from his cockpit of the port Kette in a vee formation of Bf 110s (three Ketten each of 3 aircraft).

From the left: Lt. Göring (killed on 11/07/40), Lt. Graf zu Castell (like Göring killed on 11/07/40 with III/ZG 76), Hptm. von Boltenstern (Staffelkapitän of 14 Staffel of V/LG 1, then Kommandeur of Erpr.Gr. 210, killed on 4 September 1940).

L1+XB, the aircraft of the Gruppenkommandeur, photographed from another aircraft.

Above: Uffz. W. Arndt, gunner of Lt. Altendorf (15 Staffel), sitting on the cockpit sill of their Bf 110.

Right: Lt. Krebitz of 14 Staffel and his grave (below) in Yugoslavia (1941).

The crew of Obfw. Röhring (left) and radio operator Uffz. Große (above) of 14 Staffel. Große is seen here as an Oberfeldwebel, when he flew as radio operator for Oblt. Leickhardt. Leickhardt was seriously wounded on 12 May 1940 and did not return to the Gruppe until 7 October, several days after it was renamed I/NJG 3.

L1+IL, the aircraft of Lt. Altendorf and Uffz. Arndt of 15 Staffel. An attempt has been made to camouflage the aircraft with saplings, but sitting in the open as it is, it is doubtful that this would have prevented it from being seen from above.

The crew of Fw. Lindemann and his radio operator Obgefr. Hübner. The photo is taken from a book, but it is the only known one of Hübner.

Right: Servicing the engine of a Bf 110.

England

From 12 July to 27 August V/LG 1 was stationed at a forward airfield 15 km south of Caen, near Rocquancourt. The Stab was quartered in Garcelles (top left and right), 15 Staffel in the Chateau Gouvix in Bretteville (middle left and right), and 13 and 14 Staffeln in Rocquancourt itself (bottom). Even afterward one Staffel was kept stationed at Rocquancourt until the Gruppe was disbanded on 27 September 1940.

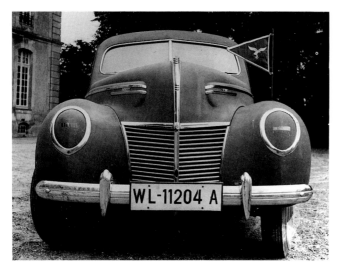

The Stab's Mercury automobile parked in front of the chateau in Garcelles with the pennant "V.Lehr.+Geschwader 1."

Recipients of the Iron Cross, First Class at Garcelles between 15 July and 5 August 1940. From the left: Fw. Kobert, Fw. Datz, Fw. Jentzsch (all of 13 Staffel), Oblt. Zobel (adjutant), Fw. Jecke, Lt. Werner, Fw. Sturm (all of 14 Staffel).

*Above and below: Burial of Fw. Würgatsch in the cemetery at Cherbourg.
After returning from a mission on 23 July 1940 his Bf 110 overturned on landing at Cherbourg airfield. Following this and similar accidents, orders were
issued for aircraft returning with battle damage to execute wheels-up landings
rather than attempt to land with the undercarriage lowered. At the back three
officers from his 14 Staffel, first from left Oblt. Junge.*

*Fw. Warrelmann of 15 Staffel photographed while sewing on his Feldwebel
(sergeant) stripes.*

Left: The approach to the Cherbourg-West airfield passed over the fort. In most cases V/LG 1 flew there (from Caen-South/Rocquancourt) and then departed on its missions over England. Right: The mole at Cherbourg and fort.

French anti-aircraft guns in the port of Cherbourg.　　　　*Obfw. Wagner with his radio operator Uffz. Heldt of 15 Staffel.*

Oblt. Weckeiser and Lt. Altendorf of 15 Staffel have something to celebrate.

Kapitän of 14 Staffel, Oblt. Junge, killed on 4 September 1940.

Above and below: More sacrifices on both sides.

Right: Hptm. Mauke with Hptm. Liensberger in the park at Garcelles. Mauke, originally a civilian pilot, was Kapitän of 14 Staffel for a short time. He subsequently fell sick and was ordered to a hospital in Germany.

Four officers of 14 Staffel in front of their quarters in Rocquancourt; from the left: Lt. Werner, Oblt. Junge, Hptm. Mauke and Lt. Eichhorn.

The aft-firing machine-gun of a Bf 110, which was operated by the radio operator.

L1+KL, crewed by Obfw. Wagner and Uffz. Held of 15 Staffel; in the left background another Bf 110.

A Bf 110 of V/LG 1 in low-level flight over the French seaside resort of Deauville.

Tail section of a Bf 110 of V/LG 1; this photo was taken while on approach to the forward airfield near Rocquancourt, south of Caen.

V/LG 1's second fatal accident at Cherbourg airfield, this time involving an aircraft of 13 Staffel. The Gruppe's loss report for 08 August 1940 stated: "Crash landing as a result of battle damage, aircraft overturned resulting in fatal injuries." Fw. Jentzsch was also buried in Cherbourg cemetery.

The aircraft of Lt. Altendorf (15 Staffel). A locomotive with tender was painted on the machine as well as the Gruppe's "Wolf's Head" emblem.

Lt. Altendorf leans back into the cockpit of his radio operator, Uffz. Arndt.

Oblt. Schnoor with Lt. Eisele of 15 Staffel.

Oblt. Glienke of 13 Staffel, to the left of him in the deck chair is his radio operator Uffz. Hoyer.

On approach to the airfield at Cherbourg. In the bottom left corner the wingtip of a Bf 110.

L1+CK of 14 Staffel. According to his logbook, between 3 June and 13 August 1940 Oblt. Junge flew 31 missions in an aircraft with these markings. On 4 September he was shot down in L1+FK. Fw. Lindemann, likewise of 14 Staffel, was killed on 27 September, also in an aircraft coded L1+CK. As a general rule, therefore, it is impossible to assign a specific code to just one crew.

Fw. Datz and his radio operator Uffz. Lämmel of 13 Staffel.

Fw. Klever of 13 Staffel.

The Bf 110 furthest from the camera wears the code L1+CK, identifying it as an aircraft of 14 Staffel.

Bf 110s of V/LG 1 on the airfield at Cherbourg. During the period 3 July to 8 August 1940 the Gruppe used Cherbourg as a staging base for its missions over England (Isle of Wight, Portland, Plymouth).

Right: Oblt. Altendorf of 15 Staffel and a mechanic take care of a minor problem.

"Shot down by own fighters" appears in Oblt. Müntefering's logbook under the date 12 March 1941, by which time he was serving with III/NJG 1. In 1940 he was technical officer, then Kapitän of 14 Staffel of V/LG 1.

Uffz. Pfaffelhuber of 15 Staffel, killed in action together with his radio opera-tor Uffz. Kramp on 09 September 1940.

Uffz. Speier of 15 Staffel. He and his pilot Uffz. Neumann failed to return from a mission on 9 September 1940. Both Speier and Neumann washed up on the French coast days later and were buried in France (two photos below).

Group photos of 13 Staffel. The first was apparently taken by Lt. Beck, the second by Fw. Datz. Each is seen on the extreme left of one of the photos, camera still in hand. Back row, beginning second from the left: Fw. Jentzsch, Uffz. Wiebe, Uffz. Busch, Uffz. Dieckmann. Sitting, from the left: Uffz. Lämmel, Fw. Meinig, Obfw. Kobert, Uffz. Seufert, Fw. Hoffmann.

Fw. Klever with his radio operator Uffz. Weller (13 Staffel). Both were wounded in air combat on 13 August 1940 and were taken to hospital in Caen after their return. Weller was left unfit to fly, while Klever was killed in action on 8 April 1944 while serving with IV/NJG 6.

Lt. Beck with radio operator Uffz. Busch of 13 Staffel. Busch was seriously wounded in air combat on 08 August 1940 (bullet wound in thigh, splinter in eye). Just five days later, on 13 August, Beck was killed in action together with his new radio operator Uffz. Hoyer.

L1+FH of Lt. Goetze and Uffz. Seufert of 13 Staffel.

Officers of 14 Staffel at Rocquancourt; from the left: Lt. Eichhorn, Oblt. Junge, Lt. Werner, Hptm. Mauke and Lt. Braukmeier.

Members of 15 Staffel on the beach at Caen ("Riva Bella"). On the far left is Lt. Altendorf and next to him Oblt. Schnoor.

The aircraft of Lt. Altendorf of 15 Staffel, identifiable by the white locomotive painted beneath the cockpit.

L1+IL photographed from L1+AL off the French coast. Both aircraft belonged to 15 Staffel.

This Bf 110 returned safely from a mission in spite of a battered wing root.

Shopping trip in France by truck. Right is Fw. Warrelmann of 15 Staffel.

The British Channel Island of Guernsey, photographed from L1+IL. The wingtip is visible at the bottom center with the letter "I".

The tail section of a Bf 110 over Riva Bella beach near Caen.

In front of the command post in Garcelles near Caen. Lt. Schultze of 13 Staffel reports for duty after returning from French captivity (he had been shot down over Vouziers on 12 May 1940). From the left: Hptm. von Boltenstern, special duties officer Oblt. Haarmann, Kommandeur Hptm. Liensberger, Oblt. Junge, Lt. Schultze, Hptm. Mauke, medical officer. Right: Lt. Schultze with Hptm. Liensberger.

Lt. Altendorf of 15 Staffel looks back into his radio operator's cockpit.

Right: Lt. Altendorf and Obfw. Wagner of 15 Staffel. They were probably using the table tennis table to shield them from the wind.

Servicing a Bf 110 of V/LG 1. The nose fairing has been slid forward for access to the four nose-mounted machine-guns, while the oil cooler of one of the aircraft's engines is being checked or replaced.

L1+EL of 15 Staffel was also flown by several crews; however, it is known from logbook entries to have been used by Oblt. Schnoor and Lt. Altendorf.

Above: Lt. Eichhorn (right) with his radio operator Uffz. Growe of 14 Staffel. Parked in the background are two Bf 110s, right L1+CK.

Right. Uffz. Busch, Lt. Bock's radio operator (13 Staffel).

Left: Fw. Datz's chief mechanic in front of Datz's aircraft L1+JH (13 Staffel). Right: Obfw. Wagner of 15 Staffel was shot down over the English Channel on "Eagle Day" (13 August 1940). Wagner, along with his radio operator Uffz. Heldt, failed to get out and went to the bottom with their aircraft.

Right: Lt. Altendorf watches the "black men" working on his machine.

Below: L1+KL, flown by Obfw. Wagner of 15 Staffel, photographed from Bf 110 L1+BR (the aircraft letter "B" is visible on the wingtip and the bottom left).

A Schwarm (flight of four) from 15 Staffel (identifiable by the fourth letter "L" in the aircraft code).

Aircraft of 15 Staffel during the return flight and on approach to land. Only Uffz. Pfaffelhuber's L1+DL can be identified.

Right: Aircraft of V/LG 1 in low-level flight off the cliffs of the Channel Coast.

Below: Bf 110s of V/LG 1. Aircraft L1+ML has light-colored fuselage sides, while the machine beyond it wears the dark green scheme on all upper surfaces.

Left: In Caen; from the left: special duties officer Oblt. Haarmann, special duties officer Oblt. Braun, unidentified, Oblt. Glienke, Oblt. Müller and Hptm. Liensberger. Right: Which lucky fellow is being waved to?

The tail section of L1+IL, which returned from a mission with seven bullet holes.

Uffz. Weller (13 Staffel), radio operator of Fw. Klever, in front of their Bf 110.

L1+AK of 14 Staffel over the Channel.

Uffz. Arndt, radio operator of Lt. Altendorf, in front of his Bf 110.

Left: On 1 September 1940 Obfw. Kobert of 13 Staffel was obliged to make a forced landing near Bilsington, Kent in L1+OH (replacement aircraft) after both engines failed. He and his radio operator Fw. Meinig escaped injury and were taken prisoner by the British. Right: Oblt. Müller, Kapitän of 13 Staffel, during the noon break.

Above and below: A rough forced landing by a Bf 110 of V/LG 1.

A communications aircraft (Bü 131) on V/LG 1's forward airfield at Ligescourt near Crecy en Ponthieu. In the background are the empty blast pens for the Bf 110s with the saplings used for camouflage moved aside. The Messerschmitts must either have been on a mission or had taxied out onto the airfield.

Above and below: Obstlt. Grabmann, the Kommodore of ZG 76 and the ex-Kommandeur of V/LG 1, with the Kapitän of 14 Staffel, Oblt. Müller, and the current Kommandeur Hptm. Liensberger.

No rest even during a short break. From the left Hptm. Liensberger, medical officer Dr. Weischer and Oblt. Müller.

A 15 Staffel mechanic carries out final checks before a mission.

Right: Conversation between Oblt. Müller of 13 Staffel and Hptm. Liensberger; in the background the flat surface of the forward airfield at Ligescourt.

Uffz. Bechthold of 14 Staffel in his L1+DL on the airfield at Ligescourt.

Right: Servicing a Bf 110 of 15 Staffel; note the home-made ladder being used by the ground crew.

Below: Fourth from the right is Lt. von Bonin, who joined V/LG 1 on 7 September 1940 and was transferred to II/NJG 1 on 24 October. Tenth from the right is Uffz. Stöber, who joined the Gruppe on 20 August 1940. This photo was taken while the pair were undergoing Zerstörer training at Schleißheim.

Right: 4 September 1940: Generalfeldmarshall Kesselring presents the Iron Cross, First Class to members of V/LG 1. From the left: Lt. Adametz (14 Staffel, KIA 15/09/40), Uffz. Köpge (Stab, KIA 27/09/40), Uffz. Brüggow (15 Staffel, POW 27/09/40), Uffz. Seufert (13 Staffel, according to his logbook he flew his last mission on 24/04/45 with NJG 3 in Ju 88 "D5+AH."

The base at Ligescourt. Camouflaged with saplings, the Bf 110s of V/LG 1 parked at the forest's edge are almost undetectable.

Above: L1+XB, the aircraft of Hptm. Liensberger, shortly before taking off from Ligescourt on 29 August 1940 (logbook: 1550-1745 hours, free chase mission over London). This was the first mission flown from Ligescourt, as the Gruppe had just transferred there from Rocquancourt one day earlier (logbook 28/8: Transfer flight Rocquancourt to Ligescourt, 1605-1650 hours)

A Bf 110 of V/LG 1. This photo provides a good view of the tire covers which were intended to protect the tires from direct sunlight when the aircraft was sparked in the open.

Right: Hptm. Liensberger and other officers of the Gruppe salute during a visit by a high-ranking officer.

6

Last Day

It was all the more disillusioning, therefore, when the crews were wakened early on the morning of 27 September as a result of an alarm. "We were told to drive out to the airfield at once," remembered Horst Brüggow. "No one really knew what was happening. People were running in all directions. There was obvious concern. There was somehow a sense of urgency. And then we realized that there was going to be a mission."

Eleven machines taxied out for takeoff. They were crewed by: *Kommandeur* Hptm. Liensberger/Uffz. Köpge of the *Stab*; Lt. Goetze/Uffz. Seufert, Fw. Bruns/Gefr. Gröbl, and Gefr. Swielik/Gefr. Welz of 13 *Staffel*; Oblt. Zobel/Uffz. Pellnat, Lt. von Bonin/Uffz. Johrden, Fw. Lindemann/Obgefr. Hübner, Uffz. Bechthold/Uffz. Koch and Uffz. Voelskow/Uffz. Schwarz of 14 *Staffel*; and Oblt. Freiherr von Gravenreuth/Fw. Reinhold and Oblt. Weckeiser/Uffz. Brüggow of 15 *Staffel*.

Only ten machines took off. Lt. von Bonin wrote (in 1988):

"In the late summer I joined V/(Z) LG 1 at a forward airfield near Caen – I believe it was Ligescourt – from the *Zerstörer* Replacement Training *Gruppe* at Copenhagen-Vaerlöse. My *Staffelkapitän* was Oblt. Zobel. I had taken part in two missions at most, during which there was no contact with the enemy, apart from anti-aircraft fire as I remember. Together with Bf 109s we flew escort for He 111s. As I recall the targets were dock facilities in the bend in the Thames. On the last mission, in which the unit was completely wiped out, I was assigned to the *Stabsschwarm* as the number four aircraft. Just before takeoff a motorcyclist roared up beneath us and waved excitedly to me, signaling that I should not take off, that I should taxi back in. I had no idea what might be going on. At the parking area

at the edge of the forest I shut down the machine and after I had climbed out I saw what was the matter. When I had taxied out for takeoff a thick branch had been thrown up and had smashed the vertical tail surfaces on one side. Then everyone waited tensely for the return of our comrades, but there was an unpleasant surprise. A number of machines straggled back to the airfield alone, some shot up, and we learned that the rendezvous over Cap Griz Nez had gone wrong. The shock at the time was great when only the battered remnants of the *Gruppe* landed and even the ground crews had tears in their eyes. The mood was miserable."

Von Bonin was then assigned to I/NJG 3 and in November 1943 became *Kommandeur* of II/NJG 1. His assessment of the Bf 110 made in 1989 is interesting:

"It was an outstanding success as a night-fighter and I didn't know any of the most successful night-fighter pilots who hadn't flown the 110. In normal flight its speed was approximately 360 kph (rule of thumb for dead-reckoning navigation: 1 minute = 6 kilometers). Of course the speed was greater at the so-called rated altitude (approx. 5,000 m), where engine output returned to near that at ground level thanks to the superchargers but where air resistance was correspondingly less. It was probably 100 kph more. It made little difference whether the radio operator had a single or a twin-barreled machine-gun. If he hit the target it was more or less good, if he missed even twin machine-guns were of no use. It was more for moral support. The '*Schräge Musik*' (upward-firing guns) was fired by the pilot, was a great thing and should have come much sooner. During my first victory with the oblique weapons I saw the glimmer rounds passing far behind the bomber. Before I attacked again with the forward-firing weapons, out of curiosity I tried again with a few shots fired with the necessary deflection, of which 2 or 3 hit. I had only intended it as a test but the bird exploded. Yes, our ammunition was in a class by itself. Someday I must really write down my recollections of the Bf 110. Without night fighting the Bf 110 really probably wouldn't have had a chance, but it was there when the night fighter arm was being built up and then did its duty to the bitter end and proved a great success."

At 9:30 AM Central European time the ten Bf 110s lifted off from the airfield at Ligescourt. What the crews did not know was that they had been sent on a feint attack. The entire formation consisted of the remnants of V/LG 1 and 13 still-serviceable Bf 110s of II and III/ZG 76, which flew escort for approximately 15 Ju 88s of I/KG 77. Indirect escort was provided by about 40 Bf 109s of I and II *Gruppen* of JG 27. The objective was to draw the British fighters into the air and weaken them to the maximum extent possible in preparation for the two big raids at noon and in the afternoon.

The weather forecast was favorable: increasing and diminishing layers of cloud over England from north to south. Ground fog over areas of southern England in the morning. Clouds forming above 8,000 meters, building and increasing throughout the day. Beneath the high cloud layer individual banks of cloud between 2,000 and 3,000 meters. Occasional light rain over the southeast of England. Area of precipitation moving from the east of England to the southeast. Over the Channel cloudy with surface fog.

The British radar stations of 11 Group issued the first warnings about the preparation, takeoff and assembly of the German formation at about 9 AM. Beginning at 9:30 the stations in Kent and Sussex began picking up the enemy incursions. 11 Group's planned reaction was to establish a barrier south of the Thames with the fighters based on airfields south and southeast of London and send them against the approaching enemy. The squadrons stationed north and northeast of London were directed to a line north of the Thames, from where they would be sent south if London was identified as the target. The following units took to the air:

9:45 AM: 12 Hurricanes of 46 Squadron from Stapleford Tawney, loiter area in the Wickford area (south of Chelmsford)
9:50 AM: 12 Hurricanes of 249 Squadron from North Weald, loiter area in the Wickford area.

9:50 AM: 12 Hurricanes of 213 Squadron from Tangmere, into the assumed flight path of the enemy.
10:00 AM: 12 Hurricanes of 17 Squadron from Debden, patrol line between Maidstone and Canterbury.
10:00 AM: 12 Hurricanes of 73 Squadron from castle Camps, as 17 Squadron.
10:00 AM: 12 Hurricanes of 1 Squadron RCAF from Northolt, to the Kenley-Biggin Hill area.
10:00 AM: 11 Hurricanes of 303 (Polish) Squadron from Northolt, as 1 Squadron RCAF.

In addition to these squadrons from airfields in the north, the following units took off from bases in the south:
9:45 AM: 11 Spitfires of 92 Squadron from Biggin Hill, to the Sevenoaks and Maidstone area.
9:55 AM: 12 Spitfires of 72 Squadron from Biggin Hill, as 92 Squadron.
10:00 AM: 12 Hurricanes of 501 Squadron from Kenley, into the area over Kenley.
10:05 AM: 10 Hurricanes of 253 Squadron from Kenley, as 501 Squadron.

After forming up over Cap Griz Nez, southwest of Calais, the closest point to England, and crossing the Channel, the German formation must have reached the English coast between Hastings and Dover at approximately 10 AM. The Ju 88s were flying at an altitude of about 5,000 meters, the Bf 110s about 500 meters higher and the Bf 109s beneath the almost solid layer of cloud at 7,500 meters.

The first RAF unit to make contact with the approaching German formation was 213 Squadron, at approximately 10:10 west of Mayfield. If followed along the formation's line of approach but was repeatedly held at bay by the Bf 110s. The Hurricanes were unable to do much against the still intact defensive strength of the 23 Bf 110s of V/LG 1 and II and III/ZG 76, which were flying in two defensive circles. Between 10:20 and 10:35 AM 1 Squadron RCAF and 303 Squadron arrived in the Reigate-Redhill-Caterham area from the northwest, followed by 253 and 501 Squadrons.

JG 27 lost one aircraft. It caught fire as a result of engine trouble and crashed near Selmeston. The pilot, Gefr. John, bailed out. He died in May 1941, shortly after being transferred from Great Britain to Canada.

At about the same time KG 77 lost two Ju 88s. The aircraft crewed by Fw. Bräutigam, Uffz. Winkelmann, Fw. Precht and Uffz. Kasing crashed onto North Ende Lodge near East Grinstead. Kasing was unable to abandon the aircraft. The other three crew members bailed out but only Bräutigam survived.

Hans-Joachim Tenholt was then an *Unteroffizier* and the observer in one of the other Ju 88s. It crashed in flames on Holly Farm near South Holmwood. He remembered:

"After we had been summoned from our quarters very early, we at first assumed that it would be another of the frequent false alarms, most of which ended at the Channel. But this time there was a detailed flight briefing, during which we were informed that London was to be attacked. My *Staffel's* target was a power station in the bend of the Thames. We formed up over Laon and rendezvoused with our escort over Cap Gris Nez. After overflying the coast the formation continued its approach to London undisturbed. No until we were in sight of London did we meet concentrated resistance, RAF fighters, light and heavy flak, barrage balloons. We flew toward London from a southeast direction, were attacked over the approaches to the city, and then turned onto a west heading. The fighter escort of Bf 110s was romping around more at the front of the formation. Our machine and another brought up the rear. We were attacked three times. The first knocked out our starboard engine, we lost speed and lagged behind the formation. The next attack followed shortly thereafter. The engine was stopped and on fire. After falling further behind we were attacked a third time. This time the port engine and wing were hit. Both were blazing fiercely, fanned by the slipstream. There was nothing left for us but to abandon the aircraft as fast as we could, because we had to expect an explosion of the tank in the wing."

Uffz. Tenholt, pilot Uffz. Schumann and gunner Uffz. Ackermann became prisoners of war. Radio operator Uffz. Memmingmann was killed.

By 10:40 AM the critical point at which the formation reversed course was drawing nearer. Meanwhile three additional fighter squadrons had arrived:

10 Spitfires of 602 Squadron which took off from Westhampnett at 10:15,
12 Hurricanes of 65 Squadron which took off from Croydon at 10:23,
12 Spitfires of 66 Squadron which took off from Gravesend at 10:25.

But it would not be these squadrons or the ones already engaged that would inflict heavy losses on V/LG 1, rather it would be 349 and 46 Squadrons, which were vectored from the loiter position near Wickford-Chelmsford, together with 73 Squadron from Maidstone-Canterbury.

Walter Grabmann, at that time an *Oberstleutnant* and *Kommodore* of ZG 76, wrote in 1987:

"The bulk of the indirect fighter escort (Bf 109s) was intercepted and engaged by British patrols after crossing the coast. By the time the bombers reached London there were guarded only by the weak *Zerstörer* forces (Bf 110s). Concentrated attacks over London by superior numbers of British fighters drew away the last forces escorting the bombers (Ju 88s). And so, for example, the 13 aircraft of ZG 76 (I led this formation myself) found themselves in a defensive circle over London for more than twenty minutes and during this time we were engaged by several British fighter squadrons. We sustained no losses while in the defensive circle. But then our fuel state forced us to break off the engagement. Finally, after the 'red lamp' of my machine's fuel indicator came on, meaning that I had just 15-20 minutes flying time left, I radioed the command 'break off, dive away,' and we peeled off out of our circle. After a steep dive I went into a shallow descent, in which the Bf 110 was faster than the British fighters. My radio operator Obfw. Walzenbach told me that three British fighters chased me. Then he said, 'They are not closing, getting smaller!' I remained in the shallow descent from 6,000 meters down to ground level and apart from occasional anti-aircraft fire was not bothered until I departed the coast. I flew low over the sea to the French coast and landed at III/ZG 76's base at Lisieux."

Grabmann remained *Kommodore* of ZG 76, which from the end of 1940 was based at Stavanger, until August 1941. He subsequently commanded the *Zerstörer* training *Geschwader* at Memmingen until August 1942. In September he went to Deelen in Holland as fighter commander of the Holland-Ruhr region. There *Oberst* Grabmann took over command of 3 *Jagddivision* in November 1943. When the war ended *Generalmajor* Grabmann was taken prisoner by the British, who held him in the reservation camp in Schleswig-Holstein and in England until his release in 1948.

Twelve aircraft of ZG 76 succeeded in disengaging from the British fighters. Only the *Geschwaderadjutant*, Oblt. von Eichborn, was shot down over the Channel:

"After the considerable losses suffered in previous missions. only about 13 machines from KG 76, including Grabmann and me, took part in the operation on 27 September. V/LG 1, which was attached to ZG 76, took part in the same mission, but when we were attacked by British fighters it formed its own defensive circle above the bombers. When one of my engines was hit and knocked out I had to try and reach the coast alone and at low-level. In spite of running attacks by British fighters I managed to get as far as the Channel. But then a cable fire broke out in the fuselage which quickly set the entire aircraft on fire. With burns on my head and hands I succeeded in setting down on the relatively calm English Channel and jumping into the water. But my radio operator Uffz. Bartmuss, who had bailed out at high speed, was killed when he struck the water. After drifting in the direction of the Atlantic in my life vest for several hours without getting any nearer the coast, in the early afternoon a fishing boat happened by. It picked me up and dropped me off in the port of Hastings. After a brief stay in a field hospital near Seven Oaks I arrived at the Royal Herbert Hospital in Woolwich. I heard the man in the next bed ask his neighbor on the left after looking at me: will that ever be a face again? That it did become one the doctors attributed to the long bath in salt water which kept the cells fresh. The only annoying thing was that at Seven Oaks they had wrapped my entire face in absorbent cotton which now had to be laboriously plucked out."

Von Eichhorn was sent to a prisoner of war camp in Canada and was released in December 1946.

The twelve crews of ZG 76 probably owed their escape to the fact that they made their break for home "just as the air was clear," as Grabmann recalled. The RAF fighters were reforming for another attack or were already attacking the second defensive circle, formed by V/LG 1. This was almost wiped out, losing seven of ten Bf 110s.

None of the survivors were able to observe what happened to the others as each was occupied with his own machine's immediate surroundings. Likewise no concrete conclusions can be drawn from the combat reports filed by the British pilots who claimed victories or shares in same. It is certain that in each case a number of Spitfires or Hurricanes attacked the same Bf 110, but not which and whose hits ultimately caused the machine to crash. Corresponding details concerning the location and circumstances of a crash are valuable clues in the identification of the machine concerned. There also are wide variations in times given. Understandably the combatants had more important things to worry about then the precise time and while one pilot might base his information on the start of the air battle, another might choose to use the end. It is therefore difficult to determine the sequence in which the seven Bf 110s were lost, however all must have gone down between 10:40 and 1:50 AM.

The crew of Oblt. Weckeiser and Uffz. Brüggow were shot down the farthest north, near Oxted on the southern outskirts of London. First Weckeiser's account:

"After overflying the English coast we were attacked by British fighters. Our formation immediately formed a defensive circle. My machine was hit in an attack by a Spitfire, after which both engines refused to accelerate.

The ignitions were shot up and as well we were losing coolant. I had to leave the circle and descended in a tight spiral, outturning the enemy fighters which attacked constantly. In one of these attacks my radio operator and gunner Uffz. Brüggow was wounded in the thigh. I made a belly landing in a field near Socketts Manor in Surrey."

Brüggow remembered:

"The strong reaction by the enemy forced us into a defensive circle. We went round, more or less disciplined, in the defensive circle for approximately 20 minutes. At first we defended ourselves very well against the attacks flown by the Hurricanes and Spitfires. I noted the departure of four of our aircraft. Naturally this had an effect on the order and battle conduct of the *Gruppe*. It also led me to ask *Oberleutnant* Weckeiser: 'Who's still in front of us?' Reply: 'There's no one in front of us, I thought they were behind us!' Soon we were ourselves hit. The left engine began to smoke, then the right too, the radiator was hit. I screamed: 'Look out, about 6 Hurricanes at 7 o'clock, break left!' Seconds later: 'Two Hurricanes at 6 o'clock, dive!' Once again I heard the sound of bullets striking the aircraft. We lost altitude, the loss of coolant caused the engines to run hot and they no longer produced normal power. All the while we were under constant attack by Hurricanes. Before we knew it the machine was unflyable. Shortly before our belly landing we were hit by another burst from a Hurricane."

No fewer than eight British pilots referred to this downing in their combat reports.

Sergeant Steward of 17 Squadron:

"My wingman and I flew into the Me 110s' defensive circle. One Me 110 veered out of the circle, I followed it but lost it from sight. I climbed back up to the others. Once again an Me 110 veered away and I was able to fire a 4-5 second burst at it. The tracer just missed the cockpit and the machine slowed down. I followed it down. Several other Hurricanes came as well. The Me 110 finally made a belly landing."

Sergeant Garton of 73 Squadron:

"At about 9:45 we sighted an enemy formation. Me 110s were circling round the bombers in line astern in an almost unbroken circle. The aircraft were dark green above and pale greenish-blue on the undersides of the wings and fuselage. I attacked the last machine in the formation,

Number 2 and Number 3 of my flight had already gone. I attacked from behind and fired two bursts, a total of 200 rounds per machine-gun. I took fire from the Me 110's gunner. After my second burst I closed to within about 90 yards or even less of the Me 110. Then I dove away to the left. When I turned again I saw that the Me 110 had left the formation and was going down. As far as I can say the aircraft crashed just south of the Redhill sector."

Pilot Officer Johnson of 46 Squadron:

"While patrolling west of Maidstone we attacked approximately 20 Me 110s. I noticed one Me 110, which was outside the formation, about 2,000 feet lower than the others. It may have been separated from the others by anti-aircraft fire. I made my first attack from above. I fired a 3 to 4 second burst from 90 to 40 yards. On my second attack, the machine was now at an altitude of only about 2,000 feet, I came from behind. Two other Hurricanes had arrived, the Me 110 was flying just above the treetops. As my ammunition was gone I veered off. The Me 110 crashed in a field 10 to 20 miles west of Maidstone. I believe I was partly responsible in bringing the Me 110 down, although it was obviously already in difficulties."

Sergeant Sellers of 46 Squadron:

"I took off at 8:55 and joined up with another squadron over our airfield. We flew to Lochford and patrolled at an altitude of over 20,000 feet. In the Maidstone sector we intercepted 20 Me 110s that were flying in circles. When the squadron attacked I detected an enemy machine behind me. I evaded by diving away steeply to the right. During this maneuver I saw another Me 110 beneath me and attacked it at an altitude between 4,500 and 9,000 feet with a two-second burst. Three other Hurricanes also attacked this machine and forced it to descend. I attacked three more times, twice from behind and once from the side. My tracer suggested that I was on target. The Me 110 came down southwest of Maidstone but it was neither destroyed nor did it catch fire."

Flying Officer Drummond of 92 Squadron:

"I had orders to patrol over our airfield. With two other aircraft I observed from our altitude of 6,000 feet approximately 12 bombers and 30 to 40 Me 110s flying at an altitude of 12,000 ft. We climbed and were attacked by Me 109s and Me 110s at an altitude of 9,000 ft. I fired a burst at a Me 109 and broke away. Then I saw a Me 110 in front

of me and I fired a burst at it from the side. Smoke came out of the starboard engine and it began to lose height. The Me 110 was then also attacked by several other Hurricanes. It landed in a plowed field just south of Westerham."

Pilot Officer Lofts of 249 Squadron:

"We ran into a formation of Me 110s which were flying in a defensive circle. Our flight leader attacked and the rest of the flight followed. I got on the tail of a Me 110 and fired a short burst at it from below. It immediately veered out of the circle and was pursued by other Hurricanes. I also followed it down and fired another burst at it. The engines were no longer running and came down near Lingfield in Surrey."

Pilot Officer Meaker of 249 Squadron:

"We attacked a large defensive circle of Me 110s from out of the sun. We went into a shallow dive and reached the opposite side of the circle. I fired a two-second burst at a Me 110, whereupon it immediately veered out of the circle. I followed it down in steep spirals. I fire two more short and one long burst of six seconds at it. The port engine was on fire, the right was smoking. A piece that looked like a landing flap fell away from the starboard wing. The Me 110 made a forced landing in a stubblefield near Horne in Surrey."

Sergeant Budzinski of 605 Squadron:

"We had been circling over Croydon for some time when we received orders to attack some Me 110s which were already engaged in a combat south of Kenley. The Me 110s were engaged with Spitfires. The Me 110s were flying in a circle and we climbed up to them. Then I spotted a Me 110 to my left. I swung to the left and attacked from behind and above. I fired off a rather long burst while closing from 200 to 25 yards. Then I dove away and immediately afterwards climbed back up to the right again. The Me 110 descended a little and turned to the right. At this height of more than 9,000 feet I then attacked in a dive from above from a range of 250 to 90 yards. I saw that the Me 110's port engine was on fire. It dove away and I could see it still just above the ground, east of Redhill but north of the rail line. Then I flew back to Croydon."

Several Hurricanes pursued the *Kapitän* of 15 *Staffel*, *Oberleutnant* von Gravenreuth, and his radio operator

Feldwebel Reinhold. The aircraft flew low over Gatwick airfield and came under anti-aircraft fire. It crashed on the outskirts of the airfield and exploded. Six British pilots made reference to the incident in their combat reports.

Flying Officer Lochnan of 1 Squadron RCAF:

"We sighted enemy aircraft and positioned ourselves to attack. I was flying above the squadron. As I was about to attack a Me 109 I was hit by machine-gun and cannon fire. Half of the aileron was shot away. I broke away and saw a Ju 88 under attack. I fired a burst at it and moved away when three Hurricanes attacked the Ju 88 and set it on fire. It crashed onto a house. I climbed before setting course for home and saw a Me 110 Jaguar. I attacked and fired off three aimed bursts at it, one from below while climbing, a second from the right which resulted in smoke coming out. Another Hurricane fired at the port engine. We were at an altitude of approximately 500 ft. I fired again when it came down towards me. The Me 110 crashed on Gatwick airfield."

Sergeant Hogg of 17 Squadron:

"We were attacked and scattered by Me 109s. I climbed up toward the Me 110s that were flying around above me and came toward and between them from the opposite direction. When I was in range I fired a two-second burst from ahead and below. The Me 110 immediately veered out of formation, took evasive action and lost height, to 5,000 ft. The Me 110 made turns to the left. I followed it and fired whenever the opportunity presented itself. Its port wing was down and I hit the starboard engine. A quantity of glycol and oil came out. A Spitfire and three Hurricanes arrived just before my attack but I was unable to observe any results from their fire. The Me 110 was now 125 feet above the airfield at Gatwick, where it crashed and went up in flames. Then its ammunition exploded. No one bailed out and the Me 110 kept firing until it crashed."

Pilot Officer Faddon of 73 Squadron:

"The enemy was sighted at roughly 9:40. He was flying in a circle of approximately 270 yards diameter. Each machine was directly behind another. We first climbed to 21,000 feet and then dived on the enemy formation, which was flying at an altitude of 16,500 ft. The enemy immediately broke formation. I attacked a lone Me 110 from behind without success. I broke away and saw another Me 110 being attacked from behind by three other Hurricanes.

I positioned myself 1,000 feet beneath the last Hurricane and waited for an opportunity to attack. The Me 110 made a half-roll which put it at my altitude. I closed from 500 yards, attacked from in front and fired continually. The Me 110 answered my fire with cannon and machine-guns. The tracers passed just over my cockpit and tail. The fire suddenly stopped and the machine went into a steep dive. The starboard engine was ablaze. The Me 110 went down from a height of about 3,500 ft. Because of the heavy haze I lost sight of it at a height of approximately 1,700 ft. As far as I can tell, the Me 110 crashed near Kenley or Croydon."

Sergeant Barrow of 213 Squadron:

"We circled in anti-aircraft fire in the Redhill sector. Then the flak stopped firing. I climbed and attacked a Me 110 from a range of 275 yards with a three-second burst. I saw pieces of the forward fuselage fly away as well as pieces of the wings. I broke away and saw another Me 110 leave the circle pursued by a Hurricane. I followed both down and when the pursuing Hurricane broke away I attacked the Me 110 from behind. I fired two three-second bursts from a range of 275 yards. When I turned away I saw black smoke streaming from the port engine. At this point another Hurricane attacked. I stayed with it and attacked from behind once again. The Me 110 crashed on the outskirts of Gatwick airfield."

Pilot Officer Hopkin of 602 Squadron:

"I took off from Westhampnett at 8:50. Then I was attacked by several Me 109s, whereupon I dove steeply and lost my squadron. I then headed in the direction of London and spotted Me 110s circling above me. I climbed to 20,000 feet and fired a short burst at a Me 110 but then lost sight of it. I descended and caught sight of it at a height of 7,500 ft. Light smoke was coming out of the starboard engine but the aircraft was under control. It was heading southwest at approximately 250 mph. Several Hurricanes were circling about it quite close but none of them fired. Then I fired a long burst from above and behind and saw the upper canopy and the fuselage around the cockpit splinter. The Me 110 then went down in a steep dive and crashed near an unidentified airfield."

Feldwebel Bruns and radio operator *Gefreiter* Gröbl of 13 *Staffel* crashed near Chelwood Gate, south of East Grinstead, after an attack by several Hurricanes. Both airmen were initially buried in Danehill cemetery, but in 1962 Gröbl was moved to the military cemetery at Cannock Chase and Bruns to the family plot in his home town of Bad Zwischenahn/Oldenburg. Excavation of the crash site in 1973 yielded some wreckage from the Bf 110. A propeller hub with one propeller blade is displayed in the Tangmere Military Museum.

The following British pilots claimed to have taken part in the downing of Bruns and Gröbl.

Flying Officer Russel of 1 Squadron RCAF:

"We climbed higher to attack the Me 110s which were flying in a defensive circle over Biggin Hill. We attacked the circle from the northeast. During this attack I was separated from the others and attacked a smaller formation of Me 110s which was flying somewhat farther south. I fired an eight-second burst at a Me 110 from close behind and its port engine began to burn. It went down in a steep dive pursued by four Hurricanes. It hit the ground near East Grinstead. Another Me 110 broke out of the circle and four of us gave chase. It crashed about 12 miles south of the first in a clearing among many trees."

Flight Lieutenant Oxspring of 1 Squadron RCAF:

"We sighted approximately 10 Me 110s flying south at high speed. The squadron attacked from the southwest, from 1,200 feet above. The squadron became split up. I sighted a Me 110 being pursued by a Hurricane and taking violent evasive action, this was 275 yards behind me. The Me 110 climbed steeply and I waited until it was in my line of fire. Then I dove on it and hit it with a full four-second burst. Its port engine caught fire. The Me 110 went down in an almost vertical spiral and hit the ground somewhere 9 to 12 miles southeast of Biggin Hill. I did not stay with the Me 110 but the other Hurricanes followed it until it crashed."

Flight Lieutenant Gillies of 66 Squadron:

"We sighted two formations of Me 110s, which were flying in staggered defensive circles, at an altitude of 20,000 feet 12 miles south of Biggin Hill. The squadron formed up, then we dove on the Me 110s from behind. They stopped circling and broke away toward the south coast. I approached a Me 110 from above and behind. When I got it in my sight I fired a five-second burst. It stalled and went down in a near vertical dive, its port engine smoking. I turned away to look for another target and did not see the aircraft hit the ground. The Me 110 had a normal camouflage finish. No fire was observed from the rear guns."

Flight Lieutenant Strickland of 213 Squadron:

"The squadron had orders to patrol at an altitude of 13,000 feet. We were scattered when a squadron of Spitfires dove on us. I joined up with two other Hurricanes. I heard from a London ground station that enemy aircraft were crossing the Channel. I flew towards Dover. There I saw approximately 12 Me 110s above me in a vee formation. I climbed towards the Me 110s and attacked the first aircraft from below. I fired a short burst but observed no effect. I turned away in the direction of London. I saw anti-aircraft fire and in it were approximately 30 Me 110s flying in a circle. There were about 50 Me 109s above them. I climbed to one side and waited for an opportunity to attack. Then my chance came and I attacked from above. I took the Me 110 completely by surprise. The Me 110 broke out of the circle and I attacked it all the way down. I hit it with two solid bursts from a height of 1,600 feet. Two other Hurricanes attacked as well. After my attack I broke away to the side and climbed on account of my high speed. I noticed that the Me 110's port engine was on fire. The Me 110's gunner, who had so far been silent, fired at me as I broke away. He hit my aircraft's radiator and fuselage. I made a forced landing with the wheels down. I later learned that the Me 110 had crashed near Whitchurch and had gone up in flames."

Pilot Officer Currant of 605 Squadron:

"We took off at 9:25 with orders to patrol over the airfield. When we climbed higher I saw a loose formation of about 14 twin-engined enemy aircraft at an altitude of 16,500 feet just east of Croydon. They were flying in a northwest direction. They were fired at by flak and were attacked by our fighters. When we were at 9,000 feet we received orders to watch out for dive-bombers over Kenley and Croydon at an altitude of 7,500 feet. We circled over both airfields. A combat was taking place between Me 110s and Hurricanes at 20,000 feet. The squadron was now ordered to climb up to the combat and support the other Hurricanes. The squadron climbed to 20,000 feet and carried out a line astern attack on a circle of 12 Me 110s which was just south of Kenley. I attacked a Me 110 from a range of 275 yards and fired a two-second burst from above and behind. Flames shot from the starboard engine. The Me 110 turned to the left and climbed higher. I raised my nose and sprayed the entire area for five seconds. I was 300 yards away. The Me 110 went down with its port engine on fire. I pursued it and kept firing from a range of 200 yards. Then my ammunition was gone. The Me 110 pulled out of its dive, stalled and dove inverted, both engines in flames, into a field near a wood and a house, three miles southwest of East Grinstead. No return fire was observed."

Squadron Leader McNab of 1 Squadron RCAF:

"I was squadron leader of 1 Canadian Squadron and 303 Squadron. After an attack on bombers we formed up and climbed to 20,000 feet, where approximately 20 Me 110s in a defensive circle were being attacked by several Hurricanes. I saw a Me 110 veer out of the circle and turn in the direction of the coast. I attacked with one other Hurricane. Finally flames shot from the port engine of the Bf 110, it rolled onto its back and crashed in flames in the area of Crowbough. I cannot give the exact location of the crash."

Feldwebel Lindemann and his radio operator *Obergefreiter* Hübner were also killed on 27th September. Their aircraft exploded in midair and the wreckage fell on the Coppice farm in Dallington near Heathfield. Hübner managed to bail out, however his parachute failed to open. Together with Uffz. Koch (Uffz. Bechthold's radio operator) and the crew of Hptm. Liensberger and Uffz. Köpge, they were buried in Hailsham cemetery, only a few kilometers from the Channel coast. Of the eleven fallen of 27th September these five lie together, and the only other German war casualty buried with them was *Feldwebel* Platt of KW 28, who was killed on 2 May 1941. Three RAF pilots claimed to have taken part in the downing of this aircraft:

Pilot Officer Lewis of 249 Squadron:

"I sighted a circle of Me 110s over the Redhill sector. I attacked a Me 110 from out of the sun and fired two short bursts. The Me 110 had followed down a Hurricane. The Me 110 belched smoke and went down in a step dive. I attacked the circle again and fired a burst at another Me 110 which went down with just one engine running, the starboard engine was on fire and the propeller was no longer turning. I repeatedly climbed back into the sun and attacked the rest of the circle. I hit another Me 110 which subsequently veered out of the circle, its starboard engine out. It turned for the coast and tried to get home. I forced it down. It went up in flames on a farm near Heathfield."

Flying Officer Sing of 213 Squadron:

"I was leading the squadron on patrol when we were scattered by Spitfires. I was subsequently unable to re-form. While searching for the squadron I saw two Me 110s

flying south. One was attacked by three Hurricanes, the other by one Hurricane. I joined up with the latter just as a third Hurricane arrived. I attacked from behind and fired at the same time as the other Hurricane, which was just above me. The Me 110 went up in flames and crashed in a field. When I broke away I observed that the other Me 110 had also been shot down about one mile away."

Flying Officer Eckford of 253 Squadron:

"At 9:30 we attacked Me 109s near Uckfield. After the fight I flew toward the coast at an altitude of 11,500 feet and saw below me a Me 110 being pursued by two Hurricanes. The Hurricanes were approximately 1,100 yards behind the Me 110. I dived steeply on the Me 110 and opened fire from a range of 275 yards. I saw that my tracer was on target. Both engines gave out white smoke and the Me 110 lost altitude. I attacked again from the left, pulled up and then attacked from the right. I closed to within 50 yards of the Me 110. The aircraft exploded and the wreckage fell in a field near Dallington."

Unteroffizier Bechthold, a pilot in 14 *Staffel*, described his experiences on 27th September:

"There was long-hoped-for flying weather on this notable day: clear sky, late summer warmth, little wind and plenty of sun. Then, early in the morning we learned that there was to be a big mission. In no time the camouflage was removed from the Bf 110s and they were prepared for takeoff. While the crews gathered for the flight briefing the mechanics completed the last necessary jobs. As well as great expectation, a certain nervousness was evident at the briefing. The low number of serviceable aircraft depressed us. Our mission order read: 'Takeoff at 9:30 AM, escort bombers into the London area.' When we returned to the dispersal I put on my flight suit and life vest and climbed into my L1+GL. (Author's note: Although he was a member of 14 *Staffel*, on this day Bechthold flew a 15 *Staffel* aircraft, identified by the last letter of the aircraft code – H for 13 *Staffel*, K for 14 *Staffel* and L for 15 *Staffel*. However, even these letters were non-standard, originating as they did from the former I (*schwere Jagd*)/ LG 1. The usual code letters for a Fifth *Gruppe* were: X for 13 *Staffel*, Y for 14 *Staffel* and Z for 15 *Staffel*.) While Werner, my chief mechanic, helped me strap in and prepare my oxygen system, I told him what lay ahead of us today and that three *Jagdgruppen* were going to join us as indirect escort. Anyone who had experienced the previous flights over London knew that it was going to be a hot day for us! Perched forward on the cockpit, giving the weapons one final check, he called to me: 'It would be ridiculous to think that everything won't go right today too, we have always had good luck so far.' Once again I became aware of how very much all of our comrades who had anything to do with the aircraft went along on our missions in spirit, kept their fingers crossed, and worried about us for the two hours we were gone. But then I could already hear the engines of the *Kommandeur's* machine running, the signal for me to start up. In a few seconds the engines of all the aircraft were roaring. My radio operator Hans Koch swung himself quickly into the machine. We were ready to go. The aircraft came taxiing out of the small niches in the forest. They all rolled one behind the other to the takeoff point, where they positioned themselves four abreast before taking off in pairs at full throttle seconds later. I was in the first flight, which was leading the *Gruppe*, with the *Kommandeur* and the adjutant. A last wave and a nod to our comrades on the ground and we were in the air.

Making a large circle, our aircraft formed up over the airfield and gradually set course to the north in closed formation. We lost much time on the way to the assembly point at Cap Gris Nez, waiting until the missing units had taken their assigned positions. Meanwhile the radio traffic became steadily heavier, the interference worse. My radio operator shook his head, often cursing. Finally he received the report: the three fighter units had arrived. We quickly climbed to 6,000 meters. Even though we had switched on our heated flight suits it was quite cold. Now and then I had to clear away pieces of ice that had already formed on the exhalation valve. At this point the huge armada of approximately 200 aircraft that had assembled over Cap Gris Nez at various levels was imposing. Only the Channel still lay before us. England's steep chalk cliffs near Dover rose up clearly from the horizon.

From now on we had to keep our eyes open. We scanned the sky in all directions. An inconspicuous dark dot in the distance could turn into a British fighter in a second. Far in the distance London hove into view. Southeast of it a large number of black dots suddenly became noticeably larger. They could only be British fighters climbing to intercept us! We tried to reach 7,000 meters more quickly in order to improve our position. Ahead of us, but even higher, our Bf 109s were already heavily engaged in fierce combats with Hurricanes and Spitfires. I heard 'Attention, attack!' and almost instantly we were engaged, but we were able to form a tight defensive circle just in time. Several Spitfires and Hurricanes tried to dive through our circle and score hits, then they attacked from the sides and below as well. Several waited above us for the mo-

ment when one of our aircraft left the circle. Coming from out of the sun, they immediately dove on this unprotected machine. Maintaining our defensive circle, we succeeded in fending off their fierce attacks; we even had chances to shoot back, without being able to observe the fate of the aircraft we hit. After about 20 minutes low fuel forced us to reform into *Schwärme* or if possible *Staffeln* for the flight back. An extremely critical maneuver began. For a brief period our rear was unprotected, for the difference in speeds between the individual machines was often quite considerable. It was often impossible to quickly close up tight to the new formation. That was my undoing.

I was just in the process of taking my place within the *Gruppe* when my radio operator opened fire and shouted to me: 'Break right, two fighters behind us!' As I turned I saw some tracer pass just to my left. The attacking fighter roared close past me without having scored a hit. We also evaded the second attacker by turning suddenly. Unexpectedly it suddenly became quiet again. I looked all around. I was quite alone. Had none of my comrades seen the attack? Had they all been attacked at the same time?

Hans reported two more attackers. This time they attacked simultaneously from below and above. My radio operator fired steadily at both. I hauled the machine around and took aim at one attacker. Hit, he veered off. But my machine had also been hit in this attack. Large black clouds of smoke blocked my view. The right engine sputtered, but the propeller continued to turn. Beneath me four new attackers appeared, Hurricanes. Now we were easy prey for them. I tried to shake them off with flat, descending turns. But then it was all over. A burst of machine-gun fire went through the cockpit. Splinters flew around, instruments failed, a heavy vibration shook the machine. I thought I heard a cry, the rear machine-gun fell silent. I blow on the back of the head stunned me. On the right side the heat was rising from the engine and fire leapt over the cockpit. Get out! I screamed. But behind me all was quiet. The canopy had long since flown away. I had to get out, I tried to rise up in my seat. But the slipstream forced me back again. My second attempt succeeded. I rolled through the flames down the wing, turning over several times. Finally I found the parachute handle, a jerk went through my body, and I was hanging beneath my open parachute swinging back and forth. All around me was relieving, endlessly deep peace. Suddenly a British fighter appeared and circled me. I flinched. Will he shoot at me? No!

Approximately 1,000 meters separated me from the earth. They seemed to have already noticed me. People hurried from all directions toward the place where I would probably land. The trees seemed to grow, a pond gave me a fright. But I floated past it and touched down. The parachute dragged me along for a few meters until I finally came to a stop in a small, hedge-lined meadow. The British fighter circled one last time and flew away. From everywhere hurried threatening, angry people, armed with agricultural tools, clubs or rifles. Luckily after I was disarmed a man in uniform arrived in time to see to my safety. Then they took me, hobbling with just one fur-lined boot, in a Jeep to the police station in Horam, five kilometers north of Hailsham. Only there did I notice my blood-streaked hair and the grazing wounds on my head and right upper arm. But the police seemed to be very concerned about me and I was given plenty to eat. Late that evening they transported me to a military unit near Eastbourne, where I was held for two nights enjoying good food, medical treatment and neutral conversations. Not until I arrived at an interrogation camp near Brighton, which I shared with twelve other shot-down comrades, did real captivity begin; close guard, absurd jobs and harassment, as well as many long, intensive interrogations which even included threats. When I was first interrogated I was greeted with the words: 'You are the last of V/(Z) LG 1, now I can cross you off! Here is the list with all your comrades and superiors.'"

Based on the RAF combat reports four British pilots were probably involved in shooting down Bechthold's machine. Pilot-Officer Patullo of 46 Squadron:

"I made an attack on a Me 110 which was flying in a defensive circle at 20,000 feet over Maidstone. I sprayed it with one burst, knocking it out of the battle and forcing it to leave the formation. Then I attacked it from behind, hit the gunner and knocked out both engines. The starboard engine caught fire and began to come off. One member of the crew bailed out then the Me 110 crashed vertically to the ground near Penhurst."

Pilot-Officer Leary of 17 Squadron:

"I separated from the squadron when we were attacked by Me 109s. I climbed to 20,000 feet where a large formation of Me 110s was flying in line astern. I waited for the rest of the squadron; meanwhile about 30 Hurricanes came from below me to attack. I joined up with them and got behind two Me 110s. I fired a two-second burst at the nearer one, whereupon it peeled off and disappeared beneath me. When I opened fire at the second Me 110 it made a tight right turn at about 120 mph. I emptied my guns from a

range of 100 to 50 yards. I observed tracer and incendiary bullets striking the fuselage and other parts of the Me 110. Then I saw the pilot or either one or two members of the crew leave the cockpit. The aircraft went into a shallow dive with engines running. I broke away as my ammunition was gone."

Flying Officer Barthropp of 602 Squadron:

"I received orders to fly to Mayfield and at 13,000 feet I detected many Me 109s above me. I went to 9,000 feet and saw two or three Hurricanes attacking a Me 110, which went down at an angle of 45 degrees. White smoke came from the starboard engine. I attacked twice from behind. The starboard engine was on fire and the machine crashed vertically into a plowed field 12 miles southeast of Mayfield. One member of the crew bailed out. I am sure that I hit the aircraft, but it had probably already been damaged before my attack."

Squadron Leader Hogan of 501 Squadron:

"I was leading 501 Squadron, which was following 253 Squadron, when we were instructed to intercept a formation of 20 Dorniers. While we were pursuing these, 25 Jaguars came down below and behind the squadron heading northwest. We received orders over the R/T to attack these, which the squadron did, but without success. They climbed quickly out of our range and I tried to reform the squadron to carry out our original instructions. As I was unable to do so by R/T I broke away alone. I joined up with a Hurricane of 303 Squadron that had attacked and damaged a Jaguar. It appeared to be out of ammunition. I fired a ten-second burst at the Jaguar and set its starboard engine on fire. One member of the crew bailed out and the machine hit the ground near Uckfield. The Jaguar exploded, the bright fire may have been caused by tracer ammunition."

While Uffz. Bechthold's machine crashed near Horam, the Bf 110 crewed by the *Gruppenkommandeur* Hptm. Liensberger and his radio operator Uffz. Köpge, flying at low-level and pursued by Pilot Officer Burton of 149 Sqn., went down in a field on the outskirts of Hailsham. Liensberger had almost succeeded in reaching the Channel, where he might have had a chance to escape.

Douglas Weller, an eyewitness, recalled in 1988:

"I was working in a field on our New Barn Farm on Station Road. The sirens wailed and I shut off the tractor.

I made my way to a deep drainage ditch to take my midmorning break. I heard the sound of aircraft engines north of Hailsham and realized that it was coming closer. Then I saw a Messerschmitt appear over the rooftops of Hailsham. I could clearly see the German insignia in the morning sunshine. At the same time I was able to observe a Hurricane, which was flying wide curve around the Messerschmitt in order to reach its flight path. I expected that a burst of MGF would follow, but that did not happen, the Hurricane kept moving in close. When it reached a position just beside and below the Messerschmitt the wingtip of the Hurricane and the tail section of the Messerschmitt touched and both broke off. The Messerschmitt hit the ground immediately after this incident and bored through a walled irrigation line and was completely destroyed. A huge pillar of black smoke rose up from the next field, the Hurricane was a blazing inferno. The pilot lay several meters from the burning wreck. His parachute had deployed but had not fully opened, and it was used to cover up the body until it was taken away."

Peter Walker was one of the first to reach the crash site; he remembered:

"I heard the sound of aircraft engines and machine-gun fire and crashes. I could not see what happened because the machine hit the ground before it reached our farm. I immediately made my way to the crash site. The pilot and radio operator were still in the aircraft in their seats. They were not smashed to pieces as was so often the case. My uncle, who had been working in that field, had jumped into a ditch. Pieces of wreckage fell al around him and he was the first at the scene of the incident. He had observed that the Hurricane had flown on for approximately 320 yards after first contacting the ground, then hit a treetop and finally crashed into a stout oak. The tail of the Me 110 was only about 100 yards from the main wreck. The machine had slight straight across the field. The engines, which were ripped from their mounts, had crashed through a perimeter fence and they came to a stop in a field behind Hamlin's mill, steaming and smoking. The crew was killed."

In 1948 Albert Hillman wrote:

"There were many air battles in September 1940, therefore it was not unusual to hear aircraft flying low over the town on the morning of that 27th September. I could no see which machines they were as they were flying so low. But suddenly a twin-engined German machine appeared above me at a height of about 75 feet. Only one engine was running, therefore the aircraft had one wing down. Close behind it was one of our fighters, but it did not shoot, it appeared that its ammunition was gone. The German aircraft flew so low that it almost touched the tall poplar trees along the rail line. Both aircraft flew over the tracks. Several moments later there was a crash. That was at 9:50 AM. I tried to learn further details and heard that the German aircraft had crashed in a field on the Mill Road and that the British one had crashed not far away near the Station Road. The latter machine went up in flames and burned out. Later I went to Simmon's field and saw the wreck of the twin-engined machine. The engines had broken off and had slid into the next field. The main part of the aircraft was badly damaged. The bodies of the two airmen had already been removed when I arrived. I spoke with one of my foremen who had seen the incident and learned that while flying along the line of trees the two aircraft had collided, whether by accident or intentionally, which caused the crash. My foreman immediately went to the spot where the German aircraft had crashed in order to see if he could do anything for the occupants, but there was nothing he could do. *Hauptmann* Liensberger showed no signs of external injuries. It appeared as if he had tried to bail out, as his parachute was partly open and his body was some distance behind the wreck. If he had been thrown out on impact he would have been thrown forward. The other poor chap was wedged in the machine."

Jack Walker, who was 28 years old in 1940, wrote in 1992:

"On behalf of the local authorities I reached the scene of the incident very quickly. The pilot was lying on the right side some distance from the wreck, still strapped into his seat. His boots were missing, but there was no sign of external injuries. The body of the gunner lay on its back some distance away. No external injuries could be seen on him either. He had also lost his flying boots, probably when he was thrown from the aircraft."

(Author's note: In 1962 Hptm. Liensberger was reinterred in the family plot in Innsbruck. An examination of the skeleton revealed that the skull was undamaged, only the lower jaw and one thigh bone were broken.)

In 1992 *Oberstleutnant* Wagner, an active pilot in the Austrian Air Force and an expert in crashes of fixed-wing aircraft, tried to reach a conclusion based on the available accounts and the three photos of the crash site:

"Based on the descriptions of the eyewitnesses it is safe to assume that the aircraft was flying at a height of approximately 20 meters. The overall damage suggests a relatively high speed. Based on the photographs I estimate this at more than 400 kph. The damage on the bottom of the tail section very clearly looks like a blunt impact from behind. This damage was very probably not caused by striking the ground, whereas the torn away upper end of the control surface (rudder balance) and the break in the area of the horizontal stabilizer-elevator and the deformation on the underside of the left rudder were. An impact that caused such damage could definitely have caused the tail section bearer to fracture, especially if it was under load from an elevator deflection. When a conventionally designed and controlled aircraft such as the Bf 110 loses its horizontal tail it immediately begins to tumble forward. Much of the damage also suggests this, especially the fact that the wing trailing edge is significantly more badly damaged than the leading edge. Theory: If the pilot of the Bf 110 noted that his opponent was one, no longer shooting, and two, drawing ever nearer, it would not have been unusual for him to try to shake him off, at least temporarily, by suddenly pulling up and simultaneously reducing speed (reducing power). When the pilot of the Hurricane realized the danger of collision he tried to avoid it by pulling up to the right. That is an almost automatic reaction by any pilot, as it corresponds to the most natural hand and arm movement. In this way he can most quickly bring the maximum force to bear on the stick. This would explain the collision and it fits with the description ('… both aircraft lurched upwards …'). The combined loads (full elevator and the simultaneous impact from behind) caused the tail section to break off, the aircraft began to pitch forward. The wingtips of the Hurricane were a known weak point. As the British pilot was also pulling hard (either to stay with his opponent or to evade), the wing was under a high upward load and it broke on collision. The high angle of attack meant that the piece of wing had to fly upwards ('… an object spun up and away …'). The Hurricane must have rolled very suddenly in the direction of the missing wingtip and at high speed was no longer controllable. After pitching forward through 270 degrees, the Bf 110 probably struck the ground tail first, then with the trailing edge of the wing, tipped further forward onto its nose, bending the cockpit area upwards (it ended up pointing rearwards). The collision with the water line must have happened after this. The rest then slid on more or less uncontrolled (see skid marks on the ground) and its final position was pure chance. As to the possibility that the pilot and his seat were tossed out of the aircraft I would say the following: the seats in combat aircraft were designed for a very high positive load (pressure from above), in most cases up to approximately 10 g. Since negative loads are encountered very infrequently, even in air combat, the entire aircraft and thus the seat is designed for about a third of this load. Loads of about 10 g were experienced both at the moment when the aircraft's wings were perpendicular to its actual direction of movement and when its tail struck the ground and caused it to pitch about that moment arm. It is therefore entirely possible that the seat belt held but that the entire seat was ripped from its mounts and was thrown through the top of the canopy. Assuming that the nose of the aircraft struck the walled support of the water line after impact with the ground, then the damage visible in the photos (nose bent upwards), the position of the two crewmembers and the witness statements match so precisely that there can be no other conclusion. Concerning the relative positions of the two aircraft: the impact of the Bf 110's rudder with the wing of the Hurricane resulted in the rudder being pushed forward, breaking off and turning itself around the point of contact into the slipstream. In doing so it struck sideways against the downward-tilted wing of the Hurricane. The upper part was bent to the right, the direction of impact has to point to the pivot point. The Hurricane had therefore already initiated the rolling movement to the right; this was halted by the impact on the right wing, the upward force causing part of the outer wing to break off. The aileron on the trailing edge of the wing may also have been damaged or possibly lost, rendering the Hurricane virtually uncontrollable in a very steep right turn. As I have myself seen a similar situation (crash of a SAAB 29 in 1969; the pilot lay in a forest clearing as if asleep next to his partly-opened parachute, although the aircraft was totally destroyed) I can imagine this course of events as the most probable. Perhaps one final comment: I do not believe that Pilot Officer Burton intentionally rammed, rather he was very close and was surprised by Hptm. Liensberger's maneuver."

There is no concrete information concerning the loss of the crew of Gefr. Swietlik and Gefr. Welz. Swietlik's body washed ashore on the French coast, Welz on the English coast near sandwich on 25 October. Had one of the two made use of his life raft, causing them to drift in different directions? We will never know. Today Welz rests in the Manston Road cemetery in Margate, Swietlik in the German military cemetery in Bourdon.

Two RAF pilots made probable reference to this loss in their combat reports

Sergeant Beard of 249 Squadron:

"While on patrol I attacked a circle of Me 110s. From an angle I fired four short four-second bursts at a Me 110. Its port engine began to falter, it lost coolant and white smoke came out. When the machine flew past me I saw flames coming from the engine. I subsequently lost sight of the aircraft. I then followed another Me 110 out to sea and fired several short bursts at it. It crashed into the sea approximately 6 miles off the coast."

Flight Lieutenant Rabagliati of 46 Squadron:

"Together with 249 Squadron, which flew in lead position, we attacked a circle of 20 Me 110s. I attacked a Me 110 from below and scored hits on its port motor. It veered off and went into a steep dive toward the sea. I followed it and attacked from behind, approximately 6 miles off the coast near Rye. While attacking I closed to within 50 yards. The Me 110 rolled onto its side approximately 60 feet above the water, struck the water with its left wing and disappeared."

By about 10:50 AM the ten Ju 88s of I/KG 77 that had made it to London (of 15 dispatched) had already reached the Channel on the flight home. It was there, near Lydd, that the third machine was lost. With hits in both engines pilot Uffz. Hartlein succeeded in ditching, but neither he nor gunner Flg. Krebs were able to free themselves from the aircraft. Bombardier Uffz. Schmidt and radio operator Uffz. Sergocki were rescued from the water and became prisoners of war. Three Ju 88s had turned back before reaching the target on account of mechanical problems and thus a total of 12 of this unit's aircraft returned from the mission.

Among the three Bf 110s of V/LG 1 which made it back from this disastrous mission was that flown by Lt. Goetze and his radio operator Uffz. Seufert. With one engine out and 44 bullet holes (according to the pilot log) it landed at 11:45 AM.

Sergeant Parsons of 66 Squadron may have been referring to this Bf 110 in his combat report, when he wrote:

"I noticed four Me 110s which broke out of the circle and turned away in the direction of the coast. I climbed higher and gave chase. I caught up with the last one before the coast. The Me 110 took evasive action by making slight turns and rising and descending. Finally I got into a good firing position on the Me 110's tail. I fired a three to four second burst and immediately closed the throttle. Then I fired at the starboard engine, which stopped after spewing out smoke and black oil. I then fired a short burst at the port engine, I had to break away as the leading Me 110 turned back and attacked me. When I broke away I saw

that the Me 110 was losing height rapidly and was flying over the coast near Beachy Head at a height of 1,100 to 1,400 feet."

Oberleutnant Zobel, who had been *Staffelführer* of 14 *Staffel* since 5 September, remembered that 27th of September:

"We fought a thirty-minute air battle over London in absolutely clear weather. Entire squadrons of British fighters came repeatedly and, heavily outnumbered, we were unable to break off the engagement."

Three weeks later, on 16 October, Zobel was seriously injured in a flying accident. After months in various hospitals it was determined that his flying career was over. Shortly before the end of the war Zobel lost an eye in an exchange of fire when American troops occupied an airfield near Munich.

Unteroffizier Voelskow of 14 *Staffel* recalled in 1988 how he experienced and survived 27 September 1940:

"I only joined 14 *Staffel* of V/LG 1 at Ligescourt for its last two missions. Only three aircraft returned from the second and last mission. I remember the panic circle we formed, that is what we called the attack circle within the unit. Hurricanes and Spitfires attacked from below and from above, out of the sun. When a British fighter got on the tail of the man in front of me, I fired a burst at him and followed it with further salvoes after he peeled off. In so doing I was out of the circle in fractions of a second. All I saw around me were smoke trails and British fighters like swarms of bees. I went into a dive at almost full throttle and reached 700 kph on the airspeed indicator. The Hurricanes could not keep up, they would have overrevved their engines. But at ground level they caught up and I did the only possible thing: low-level flight at a few meters over willows, hedges and the occasional house. As I did so I made repeated quick, steep turns very near the ground in order to give my pursuers a more difficult target. Once one of them went too high and lost sight of us under his engine cowling. My radio operator Kurt Schwarz fired at him. The Hurricane rolled to the right and I almost rammed it as I had also just made a right turn and was flying roughly parallel to a slope. Then my other two pursuers lost sight of me, they fired over the crest of the hill. I continued to stay low at maximum speed until the middle of the Channel, when Kurt Schwarz pounded on my shoulders with his fists and screamed: Let up! The Hurricanes hadn't followed us any farther, although there were still three off the coast."

Voelskow flew with the successor *Gruppe*, I/NJG 3, until 29 July 1942, when he crashed during a night takeoff.

"I had been placed in reserve and the Mosquitoes continually placed their eggs on our airfield, which they could see from above a thin layer of stratocumulus cloud in the pale light of a half-moon. I checked my Bf 110 several times to make sure that it hadn't been damage by bomb splinters. I finally got the order to take off and hurried to get to safety in the air. But up above they had apparently seen my exhaust flames and a stick of bombs exploded on the runway in front of me. I thought that I would be airborne before the first bomb craters, then I saw a black pillar appear before me. The crew for whom I was supposed to take off had landed on the darkened field with some sort of defect and had taxied into the first bomb crater in front of me. I hauled my machine off the ground at 160 kph indicated intending to immediately put the nose down again to gain speed, but over the obstacle I felt a jolt on the stick and then it went limp. That is the last I remember. The doctors had given up on me on account of my head injury, as well my leg was almost severed below the knee and had to be amputated. My radio operator Kurt Schwarz did not survive the accident."

After recovering from his injuries Voelskow was assigned to the Luftwaffe Hitler Youth and when the war ended he spent a brief period as a prisoner of war of the Americans.

On the evening of 27th September the RAF's 11 Group sent the following report to the headquarters of Fighter Command:

"The squadron under Wing Commander Beamish attacked approximately 20 Me 110s near Redhill at an altitude of about 16,500 ft. The enemy aircraft were flying in a defensive circle. 249 Squadron dove out of the sun in the opposite direction to which the enemy aircraft were circling and carried out mainly frontal attacks from a slightly higher position. 2,000 feet above the Me 110s were a number of Me 109s (exact number unknown). The leader of 249 Squadron is of the opinion that the Me 110s were bait for the Me 109s. The trick failed because of lack of initiative and desire to attack on the part of the Me 109s. Individual air battles followed, in which our pilots followed down those enemy aircraft selected as targets. 46 Squadron attacked what was left after the attack by 249 Squadron. The Me 109s did not take part in the air battle. Enemy losses: 8 Me 110s destroyed (6 over land, 2 over sea), 5 Me 110s probably destroyed, 1 Me 110 damaged. Own losses: 1 aircraft missing, 1 damaged, 1 pilot (Lt. Burton) missing, 1 slightly wounded."

Comments on this report follow. Altendorf (1940: *Leutnant* in 15/LG 1) in 1990:

"The notion by the leader of 249 Squadron that the Bf 110s were bait for the Bf 109s is exceedingly arrogant; it was clear to us that the so-called attack circle was purely a defensive circle, especially towards the end of the air battle. This was our weakness, not being laid out as 'bait' for the attacking Bf 109s. The Bf 109 was superior to the Spitfire and Hurricane anyway, but had very limited endurance and range, which severely restricted its use. Outnumbered by the British fighters, there was simply nothing else for us to do but form the defensive circle and if possible escape by diving away."

Von Bonin (1940: *Leutnant* in 14/LG 1) in 1990:

"Well, it couldn't have been like that. It is true that the 110 unit flew a defensive circle when the English approached and broke up on command when fuel ran low. Some escaped in a dive. In any case it is not true that 109s were there. It is unthinkable that 109s were nearby without intervening, for if 109s had been present they would definitely have intervened, for that was the role they were designed for. They were probably Hurricanes that did not intervene because there were already enough Spitfires there to deal with the 110 unit. The Hurricane was more likely to be mistaken for the 109 than the Spitfire, which had pointed wingtips. The report is also not credible because at that time the fighter units were still relatively strong and would never have avoided combat. It is also reasonable to ask why the English did not attack these 109s after the 110 unit had been chased away. No, I cannot take this report seriously, at least not the part with the 109s."

Grabmann (until April 1940 *Kommandeur* of V/LG 1, then *Kommodore* of ZG 76):

"The notion of the British formation leader that the Bf 110 unit was flying as bait for a Bf 109 unit is of course nonsense."

Eduard Neumann, Hptm. and *Gruppenkommandeur* of I/JG 27 (later *Kommodore* of JG 27 until April 1943, at the end of the war *Oberstleutnant* and commander of fighters in upper Italy) wrote in 1992:

"I can tell you nothing about 27 September 1940. It was one flight of fifty and each had its drama. It is no longer possible to say which *Gruppen* of JG 27 were near the *Zerstörer*. Not all the *Zerstörer* were shot down that day and all of the pilots of JG 27 returned. If things had happened as the English describe it would have been a case for a court martial. A case for the death sentence! In reality there was no 'incident,' and if there had it certainly would not have been forgotten. The war went on for a long time and episodes from the early years were overshadowed by later events. I am sorry that I cannot be more helpful. I am not satisfied with what I have written you." (From Neumann's log book: "Takeoff Guines 27/09/40, 9:30 AM, return 10:45, mission south of London.")

The former *Unteroffizier* Suschko of JG 3 wrote in 1992:

"It was another beautiful day when one had good visibility for takeoff and flying. We were supposed to escort some sort of formation to London. Just past Dover on the way home all hell broke loose in my machine. There was a jolt and suddenly my propeller feathered itself, which meant that all of a sudden there was no more thrust and I immediately fell behind the formation. Lame ducks over the Channel were easy pickings for the 'body strippers,' which was what we called the British fighters which lurked off the Channel Coast waiting for easy prey. I switched off the electrics and went into a dive in order to clear the most dangerous area as quickly as possible. In fact I made it to the airfield at Boulogne, where I made a belly landing. When I examined my machine I discovered a machine-gun hit in the knob of the throttle lever. This contained a toggle switch with which one could adjust the propeller pitch electrically. Others in the formation had seen a number of Spitfires pass beneath us heading the other way and said that they had pulled up and taken potshots at our formation. I of all people had to take such a stupid hit." (Log book: 27/09/40, takeoff 9:25 AM Boulogne, return 10:40, fighter sweep south of London.")

It is quite possible that the aircraft 600 meters above the Bf 110s were Spitfires and Hurricanes and were mistaken for Bf 109s. With their limited endurance the latter had probably already broken away and were no longer in this area. None of the detailed combat reports by the British pilots make any reference to Bf 109s being seen.

The British claimed 34 victories (1 Ju 88, 3 He 111s – probably misidentified Ju 88s, as no He 111s were involved – 5 Bf 109s and 25 Bf 110s). Actual German losses were 3 Ju 88s, 1 Bf 109 and 8 Bf 110s, a total of 12 aircraft altogether.

The German side claimed to have shot down 29 Hurricanes and Spitfires. Actual British losses were 11 aircraft, 7 Hurricanes and 4 Spitfires. Another 13 Hurricanes and 6 Spitfires landed with varying degrees of serious damage.

The Ic of the Luftwaffe Operations Staff issued the following situation report on this first of three attacks on 27th September:

"As a result of the bad weather only 9 bombers with fighter escort were able to attack London. The effect of the bomb strikes could not be observed on account of poor visibility, occasional solid cloud layers and strong defenses. Some of the bombs burst near the big power station in Battersea Park. Several air battles took place in the area around London and to its south."

Oblt. Haarmann, staff officer of V/LG 1, wrote in 1940:

"27th September was a black day for the *Gruppe*, when the rest of the old *Gruppe*, except for Zobel, failed to return. Liensberger is now gone too. The transfer order came on the 29th and since that time we traveled around the world until we finally set foot in the southern part of the Reich, for the time being. I was maid of all work, for the *Gruppe* was completely finished. As well it happened that our Zobel had a flying accident, which looked very bad. But thank God he was enormously lucky. Thus the last officer left the *Gruppe*, with the exception of us old fogeys."

In fact after the 27th September there were only two crews left who had been with the *Gruppe* prior to the start of the French campaign in May 1940: *Feldwebel* Jecke (still in hospital) and radio operator *Unteroffizier* Schmergal of 14 *Staffel* and *Oberleutnant* Zobel with radio operator *Unteroffizier* Pellnat. The others had been killed, wounded or captured and as well several had been transferred. Some of the wounded resumed flying in the night-fighter arm following their recovery. The personnel who had come from the *Zerstörer* Replacement Training *Gruppe* had suffered equally heavily. Of twelve crews assigned to the unit before the end of operations over England to make good losses, nine failed to return from combat sorties.

With the shortage of machines and flight personnel improvisation had to be stepped up until the end of September. Only two to four aircraft were on strength with each *Staffel*. Following the death of Oblt. Müller, the *Kapitän* of 13 *Staffel*, on 15 September, that *Staffel* was left with just one officer, Lt. Goetze.

The *Kapitän* of 14 *Staffel*, Oblt. Junge, was killed on 4 September. As this *Staffel* was also now left with no officers, *Gruppenadjutant* Oblt. Zobel assumed command.

Following the departure of the *Kapitän* of 15 *Staffel* to join the night-fighters, at the end of August the unit was given to Oblt. von Gravenreuth from the replacement training *Staffel* at Vaerlöse. He was senior to Oblt. Weckeiser, who had been flying with the *Staffel* since 1938. Von Gravenreuth was killed on 27 September 1940, while Weckeiser became a prisoner of war on the same day after a forced landing in England.

Lt. von Bonin (seen here as a Hauptmann and Kommandeur of II/NJG 1) of 14 Staffel; he did not take part in the mission of 27 September on account of a mechanical problem with his aircraft.

Oblt. von Eichhorn, adjutant of ZG 76. He took part in V/LG 1's mission on 27 September 1940 together with several aircraft of his Geschwader. Von Eichhorn's was the only aircraft of ZG 76 that failed to return, as he ended up ditching in the Channel. He was rescued by the British and returned to Germany in 1946 from captivity in Canada.

Right, Uffz. Bechthold of 14 Staffel. His aircraft was shot down over England on 27 September 1940. Bechthold's radio operator Uffz. Koch was killed, while he himself managed to parachute to safety and was taken prisoner.

The only existing photos of Oblt. Freiherr von Gravenreuth. On 7 August 1940 he joined 15 Staffel of V/LG 1 from the Zerstörer Replacement Training Staffel at Copenhagen-Vaerlöse. After a familiarization period he took over the Staffel from Oblt. Schnoor (on the left in each photo), who had secured a transfer to night fighters. Von Gravenreuth was killed on 27 September 1940.

Fw. Lindemann of 14 Staffel and his radio operator Uffz. Hübner came to grief on that catastrophic day for V/LG 1 – 27 September 1940. One member of the crew was seen attempting to bail out, however the Bf 110 exploded in midair.

Gefr. Swietlik of 13 Staffel and his grave in France. He and his radio operator Gefr. Welz managed to reach the Channel after the mission on 27 September, but then the aircraft must have crashed somewhere over the water.

Hptm. Liensberger and his radio operator Uffz. Köpge were also killed in action on 27 September 1940. The photographs of the graves of the fallen of V/LG 1 who died that day and who were buried in the cemetery at Hailsham, Sussex were taken shortly after the war.

On 27 September Oblt. Weckeiser and his radio operator Uffz. Brüggow (15 Staffel) made a successful forced landing in England after both of their aircraft's engines were hit.

The crew of Fw. Bruns and radio operator Gefr. Gröbl were shot down and killed near East Grinstead on 27 September 1940

The remains of the Bf 110 of Hptm. Liensberger and Uffz. Köpge just south of the town of Hailsham on 27 September 1940. In spite of the existing reports, the events that led to the crash must include a measure of speculation: the Bf 110 tried to reach the Channel, only 10 kilometers away, at low-level, closely pursued by a Hurricane. The Bf 110 pulled up in an attempt to shake off its pursuer. The Hurricane was unable to avoid the climbing Messerschmitt. The starboard wingtip of the Hurricane struck the starboard fin and rudder of the Bf 110. The entire tail section of the Bf 110 and the starboard wingtip of the Hurricane immediately broke off, whereupon the Bf 110 pitched forward and struck the ground. The crippled Hurricane was sent into a right turn by the collision and struck a tree.

7

V./(Z)LG 1 Becomes I./NJG 3

When seven of the unit's last ten aircraft failed to return from England on 27th September, it marked the ultimate end of V/LG 1. *Hauptmann* Peters, who arrived from ZG 2 two days later, was placed in command of the *Gruppe* for several days, and it was he who signed the last and longest casualty report submitted by the *Gruppe*. On 1 October the unit was renamed I *Gruppe* of *Nachtjagdgeschwader* 3 (I/NJG 3). 13, 14 and 15 *Staffeln* of the disbanded *Zerstörer-Gruppe* became 1, 2 and 3 *Staffeln* of the night-fighter *Gruppe* I/NJG 3.

The transfer from the forward airfield at Ligescourt to Germany began on 5 October. At 11:20 AM the unit departed for Brussels and from there at 2:30 PM for Cologne. On the 10th the unit moved on to Ingolstadt and on the 16th to Memmingen.

Just as V/LG 1, which had evolved from I Heavy Fighter *Gruppe* of *Lehrgeschwader* 1, had been one of the first *Zerstörer-Gruppen* to be formed, now I/NJG 3 became one of the first night-fighter *Gruppen*. The building phase with the arrival of new crews lasted several weeks. Conversion and familiarization training was carried out at several airfields, such as Stuttgart-Echterdingen or Königsberg under *Gruppenkommandeur* Hptm. Radusch, adjutant Hptm. Knoetzsch and *Staffelkapitäne* Hptm. Peters (1 *Staffel*), Oblt. Jüsgen (2 *Staffel*) and Oblt. Sauer (3 *Staffel*). At Vechta, the unit's base as of December 1940, the unit was rejoined by Lt. Leickhardt, seriously injured on 11 May, Fw. Warrelmann, who had crashed on 11 August, and the crew of Lt. Altendorf and Uffz. Arndt, who had been assigned to retrain on bombers at the beginning of September.

While the second and third *Staffeln* remained at Vechta, the first was transferred as an independent *Staffel* to X

Fliegerkorps. On 5 February 1941 it flew via Cologne, Echterdingen, Neubiberg, Treviso and Foggia to Gela on Sicily. On 27th May it moved on via Greece, with temporary action from Athens, Argos and Crete to Derna in Africa. Its missions were fighter sweeps over the Mediterranean and armed reconnaissance in search of British convoys. Sometimes missions were flown with a *Staffel* of JG 26 under *Oberleutnant* Müncheberg.

The *Staffel* lost three crews during its operations in the Mediterranean theater. On 9 March the aircraft of Oblt. von Weegmann and radio operator Uffz. Banser crashed off Gozo, an island near Malta. At the time *Staffelkapitän* Hptm. Peters wrote to Banser's father:

> "Unfortunately I can only tell you that even those of us who took part in this flight are unfamiliar with the details of this incident, for it all happened very quickly, and as the crash took place on enemy territory we could not fly back for a closer inspection. All that we saw was a large pillar of fire suddenly appear beside us and pieces of aircraft flying about. In my personal opinion there is little hope that the crew was able to abandon the aircraft beforehand. I can tell you that the precise timing of the accident was 7:15 AM on 9 March 1941."

The *Staffel* had previously attacked Valetta airfield on Malta and was flying low over Gozo on its way home. After reaching an altitude of approximately 600 meters it was bounced out of the sun by three British fighters. One of Peters' engines was hit and knocked out. Peters radioed that he was going to fly back to the base at Gela, Sicily alone. Two of the three

British fighters broke off their attacks on the one-engined Bf 110 and flew away. The pilot of the third positioned himself alongside Peters and waved. Peters waved back. The British aircraft stayed with the German machine until it had reached the coast of Sicily.

On 14 June the crew of Oblt. Obermayer and Fw. Mertens attempted to ditch in the Aegean Sea north of the island of Thera, it is though because of engine trouble. The attempt went awry and the crew went down with their Bf 110. Four days later on 18 June Fw. Pliberscheck and his radio operator Gefr. Leithner were killed in a takeoff crash at Argos airfield in Greece.

On 28 September 1 *Staffel* was transferred back to Vechta to join the other two Staffeln of the *Gruppe*; its route took it to Saloniki, Belgrade, Wiener-Neustadt, and Erfurt. During the period that 1 *Staffel* was in the Mediterranean, from February to September 1941, the remaining two *Staffeln* concentrated their efforts on practice night-fighter flights.

During the period in question, for example, the crew of Lt. Goetze and Uffz. Seufert of 2 *Staffel* completed 78 flights, including 18 night sorties, on 12, 24 and 31 March, 8, 9, 16 and 18 April, 12 May, 13 June from Vechta, on 15, 20, 25 and 26 July from Oldenburg and on 1, 3, 14 and 20 August from Vechta again. Lt. Goetze and Uffz. Seufert were the only crew to have returned from all their missions with V/LG 1 since the first mission against France on 10 May 1940 and went on flying until the end of 1942. Goetze then retrained on the Bf 109 and was killed in a tragic accident on 10 January 1944 while serving with III/JG 11. Seufert flew his last mission in a Ju 88 of I/NJG 3 on 24 April 1945. He survived the war.

In October 1941 Hptm. Knoetzsch, the former adjutant, relieved Hptm. Radusch as *Gruppenkommandeur*. The *Gruppe* was affected by a number of reorganizations and redesignations during the remaining war years. For example in October 1942 4/NJG 2 was renamed 2/NJG 3. Elements of the old 2 Staffel went with *Staffelkapitän* Oblt. Altendorf to I/NJG 4.

Of the 25 members of V/LG 1 who were still with the *Gruppe* or in hospital after the missions over England in 1940 and who were taken into I/NJG 3, eight were killed by the end of the war, five were discharged on account of wounds suffered. Not until 1946 did the last eleven return home after six years in prisoner of war camps in Canada.

The loss of seven of the last ten aircraft committed on 27 September 1940 spelled the end for V/LG 1. Here Oblt. Altendorf of 15 Staffel is seen packing on the airfield at Ligescourt. Note the aircraft's white-painted nose, a feature also seen on the Bf 110 of Oblt. Weckeiser (also of 15 Staffel) which force-landed in England.

The remnants of V/LG 1 transferred from France to Germany (Cologne, Ingolstadt, Memmingen, Stuttgart-Echterdingen, and weeks later to Vechta). Here aircraft of the unit are seen over Echterdingen during the flight home.

Bf 110s of V/LG 1 (or already I/NJG 3?) on an airfield near Cologne; the aircraft on the right still has the white nose used by 15 Staffel during operations over England.

Above and right: The remnants of V/LG 1 have arrived at Stuttgart-Echterdingen airfield. Third from the left is special duties officer Oblt. Braun, 4th Hptm. Peters ("placed in command of the Gruppe" after 27/09/40), 8th Lt. Schmidt of 13 Staffel, far right special duties officer Oblt. Haarmann.

Left: The first Kommandeur of I/NJG 3, the night-fighter Gruppe formed from the remains of the disbanded Zerstörergruppe (V/LG 1), was Hptm. Radusch (left). In 1987 he wrote: "My memory is too poor to be able to provide details. Bear in mind: I had to introduce three different Zerstörer-Gruppen into night fighting (V/LG 1 was the 2nd) and then led three night-fighter Geschwader, and therefore in remembering some things get mixed up." On the right of the photo Hptm. Peters in the officers' mess at Vechta. Right: At the beginning of 1941 I/NJG 3 was handed over to Hptm. Knoetzsch (far right) from Hptm. Radusch. To the left of Knoetzsch are the three Staffelkapitäne Oblt. Sauer (3 Staffel), Oblt. Jüsgen (2 Staffel) and Hptm. Peters (1 Staffel).

The Stab of I/NJG 3 at Vechta.

3 Staffel of I/NJG 3 at Vechta. From the former V/LG 1 in the first row: 2nd from left Fw. Warrelmann, 5th Lt. Goetze.

Left: Officers' mess at Vechta. Right: Officers of the Stab of I/NJG 3; second from the left is special duties officer Oblt. Haarmann, next to him on the right is medical officer Dr. Weischer (previously served with V/LG 1).

Telephone switchboard in I/NJG 3's command post at Vechta.

Second from the right is Lt. Leickhardt (ex 14 Staffel), next to him Lt. Goetze (ex 13 Staffel) and a special duties officer (ex Stab V/LG 1).

I/NJG 3's command post at Vechta; from the left: Oblt. Jüsgen, Lt. Leickhardt, Kommandeur Hptm. Knoetzsch and special duties officer Oblt. Haarmann.

Muster on the airfield at Vechta. From the right: Hptm. Schwab, Lt. Leickhardt and Hptm. Emmerich.

Above and below: Bf 110s of I/NJG 3 at Vechta. Some of the aircraft, which have been resprayed black overall, already wear the new unit code "D5" although most still have the old "L1" worn on machines of V/LG 1. According to the logbooks of Lt. Altendorf and Uffz. Arndt, on 12/10/41 their aircraft still wore its old code L1+EL, then on 21/10/41 the new D5+EL.

Left: Lt. Goetze (ex 13 Staffel) and Lt. Altendorf (ex 15 Staffel), now both members of 3 Staffel of I/NJG 3. Right: In front of the command post at Vechta. From the left: Hptm. Peters, Kapitän of 1 Staffel, Kommandeur Hptm. Knoetzsch, special duties officer Oblt. Haarmann.

Left: A game of table tennis; second from the left is Lt. Altendorf, fourth Kommandeur Hptm. Knoetzsch. Right: Members of 2 Staffel; from the left: Uffz. Schwarz (Fw. Voelskow's radio operator), Uffz. Nicke, Fw. Voelskow, Fw. Jecke and Uffz. Dierkes.

Left: Uffz. Große and Uffz. Schwarz in front of Fw. Voelskow's L1+JK (Schwarz was Voelskow's radio operator). Right: Gathering of Leutnants from 2 Staffel in the officers' mess at Vechta at the end of 1940; 2nd from the left Lt. Linnemann, then Lt. Goetze, Lt. Leickhardt and Lt. Altendorf. All except Linnemann came from V/LG 1

On the firing range at Vechta. On the left is Oblt. Milius, next to him Oblt. Altendorf. Second from the right is the medical officer, who had served with V/LG 1 in 1940.

Right: Members of the Stab of I/NJG 3 at lunch. Fourth from the left is special duties officer Oblt. Haarmann.

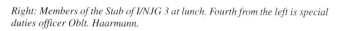

Below: Uffz. Große, who flew with Lt. Leickhardt, next to their aircraft D5+YB (Stab I/NJG 3).

Left: Crash site of the Bf 110 crewed by Lt. Schmidt and radio operator Uffz. Weniger (this crew had joined V/LG 1 in September 1940) of 3 Staffel which went down near Vechta on 23 March 1941. The casualty report declared: "Killed in crash while taking off on night-fighter mission."

Below: On the left the crew of Uffz. Große and pilot Lt. Leickhardt (Stab I/NJG 3, seen here while serving with I/NJG 5 at Stendal). Große lost an arm during a mission on 25/02/44, Leickhardt was killed on 23/02/45.

Two aircraft of I/NJG 3, L1+LK of 2 Staffel and L1+BL of 3 Staffel.

Ground crew of 3 Staffel with battery charging equipment.

Several Bf 110s of I/NJG 3. Trees have been painted on the buildings in the background in an attempt to camouflage them.

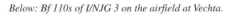

Left: Airfield buildings disguised as homes; the gabled roofs were installed for camouflage only.

Below: Bf 110s of I/NJG 3 on the airfield at Vechta.

Special duties officer Oblt. Haarmann (right) "in pleasant company."

Right: The Staffel emblem of 1 Staffel of I/NJG 3 (ex 13 Staffel of V/LG 1) during operations in the Mediterranean theater (Sicily, Greece from 05/02/41 to 28/09/41). This Staffel was employed as an independent unit while 2 and 3 Staffeln remained at Vechta.

Below: Bf 110s of 1 Staffel of I/NJG 3 over Gela, Sicily.

Commanding general Geisler visits 1/NJG 3 at Gela, Sicily on 20 March 1941. Second from the right is Staffelkapitän Hptm. Peters.

Above: The aircraft of Hptm. Peters (L1+CH) over the coast of Sicily.

Right: Hptm. Peters with Oblt. Müncheberg, who commanded a Staffel of JG 26 which was also based at Gela. Müncheberg was later killed while serving with JG 77 (23/03/43).

Below: L1+CH on the airfield at Gela. The aircraft's tires as well as its entire canopy were covered with tarpaulins for protection from the heat.

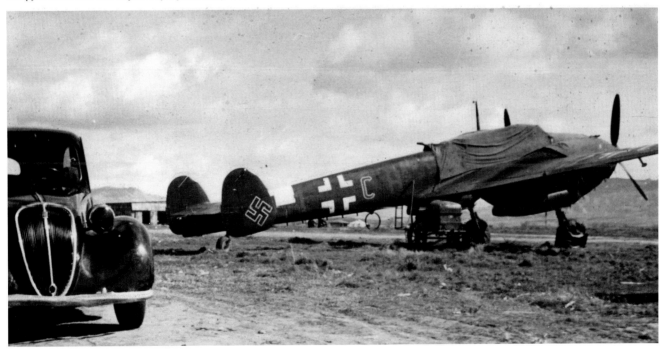

Above: In front of the command post at Gela. From the left: Fw. Wiebe, Hptm. Peters, Fw. Schmergal, and special duties officer Oblt. Braun (all came from V/LG 1).

Right: Hptm. Peters with Lt. Heinz Schmidt. The other Lt. Schmidt, first name Ernst (both came from 13 Staffel of V/LG 1), was killed in a crash near Vechta/Oldenburg on 23/03/41.

Below: Hptm. Peters with radio operator Uffz. Kohrt in their L1+CH prior to takeoff.

Left: Under the palms of Sicily; 1st from left Hptm. Peters, 3rd Fw. Busch, 7th Fw. Klever (all former members of V/LG 1). Right: Four former members of V/ LG 1 serving with 1/NJG 3 on Sicily, all wearing the Wound Badge and the Iron Cross, First Class won in operations over France and Great Britain in 1940. On the far left is Fw. Wiebe (shot down, wounded, captured by the French on 12/05/40), 3rd from the left Fw. Klever (wounded on 13/08/40), 4th and 5th Obfw. Jecke and his radio operator Uffz. Schmergal (both wounded on 15/08/40).

A Bf 110 of I/NJG 3 is prepared for takeoff.

Wearing life vests, Hptm. Peters and radio operator Uffz. Kohrt board their Bf 110 in preparation for a mission.

An aircraft of I/NJG 3 over the Mediterranean.

Bf 110s of 1 Staffel at Gela. In the deck chair on the far right is Hptm. Peters.

Presenting the Iron Cross, Second Class to members of 1 Staffel of I/NJG 3 at Gela. Above: from left: 2nd and 3rd Fw. Klever and radio operator Fw. Wiebe, 5th Hptm. Peters, next to him Fw. Busch (former members of V/LG 1). Photo Below: Far left Hptm. Peters, far right Fw. Klever; Klever, Busch and Wiebe had already earned the Iron Cross, First Class during V/LG 1's operations over Great Britain in 1940.

Group photo of 1/NJG 3 in Sicily. The only ex-members of V/LG 1 who can be identified are Fw. Schmergal (4th from left), Fw. Jecke (8th from left) and Fw. Busch (1st from right).

Group photo of German and Italian servicemen taken at Gela, Sicily. Fifth from the left is Hptm. Peters, 5th from the right Fw. Jecke and behind him his radio operator Fw. Wiebe.

Right and two below: L1+BH, the aircraft of Obfw. Jecke and his radio operator Fw. Schmergal, after a forced landing near Tripoli in the summer of 1941.

L1+DL, crewed by Lt. Altendorf and his radio operator Uffz. Arndt, near Werneuchen/Berlin on 19/08/41. In 1997 Arndt remembered: "During a mission over Berlin a Russian bomber was shot down by flak in our immediate vicinity, but our machine was also hit and an engine was knocked out. Altendorf wanted to land at the airfield at Werneuchen. Shortly before the intended landing he noticed that one tire was flat. He attempted to pull up and go around but was unable to do so with just one engine running. We crashed in a field about 100 meters from the airfield."

Above: In this view the supplementary armor-glass panel in front of the windscreen of this Bf 110 is clearly visible.

Something to celebrate. Empty glasses wait to be filled. Second from the left is Obfw. Jecke, fourth Fw. Voelskow and sixth his radio operator Uffz. Schwarz. In 1994 Voelskow could no longer remember why he was on crutches. Schwarz was later killed in a serious accident in which Voelskow lost a leg.

Right: This drawing by Oblt. Seipp is supposed to depict Oblt. Altendorf.

L1+IL, the aircraft of Fw. Warrelmann. The first four victory bars represent victories gained during the Polish campaign of 1939 while serving with V/LG 1.

3 Staffel barracks at Werneuchen; on the right is Oblt. Altendorf.

Left: I/NJG 3 ground crew at Werneuchen. Second from the left is Obfw. Jecke. Right: The command post at Werneuchen. On the far right in the first row is Fw. Arndt, while second from the right in the back is Fw. Voelskow; both were former members of V/LG 1.

The crew of Oblt. Altendorf and his radio operator Fw. Arndt of 3 Staffel of I/NJG 3 (formerly of 15 Staffel, V/LG 1) seen climbing into their aircraft.

Left: View forward from the radio operator's cockpit in the Bf 110. Right: I/NJG 3's "manufacturing plant" for Bf 110 models. Apparently there was a great demand for such models.

Left: Parade marking the departure of I/NJG 3's 3 Staffel from Vechta after the unit was transferred to I/NJG 4 at Laon/Athies in France. With the base drum Oblt. Altendorf, with the smaller drum Fw. Schmergal; behind and to the right of Schmergal is his pilot Obfw. Jecke (all came from V/LG 1). Right: Far left Oblt. Altendorf, far right Obfw. Jecke, photographed prior to a mission.

Filling the oxygen bottles of a Bf 110. This servicing truck was also used to top up the machine's supply of compressed air (for operation of the undercarriage).

Staffelkapitän Oblt. Altendorf reports 3 Staffel of I/NJG 3 ready for inspection. Both the wall of the hangar in the background and the apron have been camouflage-painted.

Above and below: The crew of Oblt. Altendorf and Fw. Arndt after returning from a mission over the English Channel on 12/02/42, part of "Operation Cerberus." On this day the battleships Scharnhorst and Gneisenau and the heavy cruiser Prinz Eugen made a dash up the Channel from Brest to Wilhelmshaven.

Mechanics check the radiator of a Bf 110.

The port undercarriage leg of this Bf 110 (L1+IL) has collapsed.

All of the stations used by V/LG 1 as well as its successor Gruppe I/NJG 3 were displayed on the walls of the mess – Neufchateau, St. Marie, Le Mans, Alencon, Rocquancourt, Crecy, (after renaming) Cologne, Ingolstadt, Memmingen, Stuttgart, Vechta, Werneuchen (Berlin), Oldenburg. Standing at the end of the table, Fw. Schmergal (ex 14 Staffel, V/LG 1) has something to say.

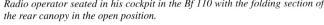

Radio operator seated in his cockpit in the Bf 110 with the folding section of the rear canopy in the open position.

A mechanic removes the cover from the cockpit of a Bf 110 prior to a mission.

Above: Aircraft of I/NJG 3 over the snow-covered landscape of Vechta.

Right: Members of the ground crew filling ammunition belts.

Below: Bf 110 of I/NJG 3 during the flight back to Werneuchen near Berlin.

Göring visits the Gruppe. Second from the right is Fw. Arndt.

Kommodore of NJG 3 Obstlt. Lent congratulates Fw. Schmergal of 2 Staffel.

Last handshake from the mechanic before taking off on a night mission.

In front of and on the empennage of L1+KH, from the left Lt. Clausnitzer, Oblt. Milius and Oblt. Altendorf.

Ground crewman at the servicing truck which supplied oxygen and compressed air.

This page and opposite: Bf 110s of I/NJG 3.

Two photographs of L1+BL of 3 Staffel. As was the case in the predecessor unit V/LG 1, the crews of I/NJG 3 often flew aircraft other than their own, even of other Staffeln. For example, according to their logbook, during the period from December 1940 to October 1941 the crew of Lt. Goetze and Uffz. Seufert flew sorties in L1+BK, HK, DK, FK, KK, AK, DL, CK, HH, KL, GK, JK, and MH – in the order that the flights were made.

Left and two below: Fw. Voelskow days after the serious accident in which his radio operator Uffz. Schwarz was killed. Voelskow sustained serious head injuries and his left leg had to be amputated below the knee. Sitting by his hospital bed is his mother. The brief note in the official casualty report: "Crashed while taking off on a night sortie."

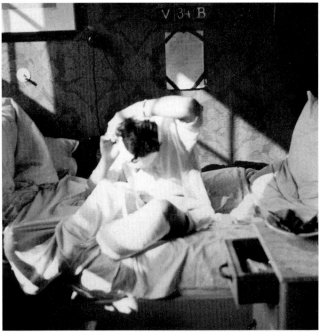

Left: Kapitän of 3 Staffel, I/NJG 3 Oblt. Altendorf seen shortly before takeoff. Note the supplementary armor-glass panel in front of the windscreen.

Bf 110s equipped with the Lichtenstein SN 1 airborne search radar.

The crew of Obfw. Jecke (right) and his radio operator Fw. Schmergal (left) in conversation with Lt. Witzleb.

Above and two below: From the logbook of Oblt. Altendorf/Fw. Arndt: "15/10/42, mission from Laon/Athies, 2148-2400 hours. At 2246 hours shot down a Halifax II near Waterloo south of Brussels." In 1997 Arndt remembered: "It was a so-called 'pathfinder,' which was virtually unarmed and dropped only target markers, called 'Christmas trees.' It was on its way home and we forced it down. To my knowledge the crew of this machine had no parachutes and therefore could not bail out. The Halifax turned like an aerobatic machine in an attempt to escape, but did not succeed."

Checking and aligning the four machine-guns of the Bf 110, which were located under the nose cowling.

Night takeoff by I/NJG 3.

Bf 110s of I/NJG 3 wearing the new unit code D5, which was introduced in November 1941. In the foreground is D5+DK and behind it D5+KK.

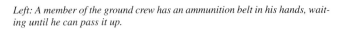

Left: A member of the ground crew has an ammunition belt in his hands, waiting until he can pass it up.

Above: I/NJG 3's 3 Staffel on parade. Fourth in the back row is Uffz. Dierkes, 2nd in the second row is Fw. Voelskow, 1st in the first row Obfw. Jecke wearing the Spanish Cross on his right breast; all were ex-members of V/LG 1. Only four members of V/LG 1 flew in Spain: Datz, Grabmann, Jecke and Schob.

2 Staffel of I/NJG 3.

Pilots at Vechta after returning from a mission over the Channel. Third from the left is Oblt. Altendorf, first from the right Uffz. Friedrich, third Uffz. Schwarz (all came from V/LG 1).

I/NJG 3 at readiness stations. In full combat gear, the airmen seek diversion in games, however the order to take off could come at any minute.

Bf 110 of I/NJG 3 in front of a hangar on snow-covered Vechta airfield.

Airfield camouflage is visible behind this Bf 110.

Two above and right: I/NJG 3 celebrates Christmas at Vechta. Above left: Kommandeur Knoetzsch addresses the Gruppe, to the right of him is Oblt. Altendorf. Above right: Oblt. Altendorf's turn to speak, note the happy faces. Second from the right in the foreground is Uffz. Schmergal. Right: Oblt. Altendorf unwraps a Christmas present. Foreground, from the left: Uffz. Friederich, Obfw. Jecke, Uffz. Schwarz.

Above: A Bf 110 of I/NJG 4, to which elements of 3 Staffel of I/NJG 3 were transferred at the end of September 1942. The unit's aircraft wore the code 3C (for example on 09/10/42 Altendorf flew 3C+EK) as well as G9, as in this photo. 3C was also used by NJG 5, while G9 was sometimes used by NJG 1. As one can see, keeping track became increasingly difficult.

Right: Two Bf 110s over the Baltic. The lighthouse on the right suggests that they are near the coast.

This Bf 110 has been raised on inflatable rubber bags, probably following a forced landing.

Right: The crews had to and did depend on the ground crews.

Above and below: Aircraft of I/NJG 3 on the airfield at Werneuchen/Berlin in 1941.

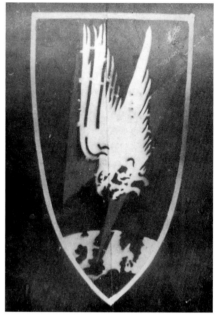

The emblem of all German night-fighter units, the "England blitz", usually applied on both sides of the fuselage beneath the cockpit.

The emblem of the German night fighter arm until the end of the war. Everything began with the "Wolf's Head" of Zerstörergruppe II/LG in 1938, followed by I/(schwere Jagd)LG 1, then V/(Z)LG 1.

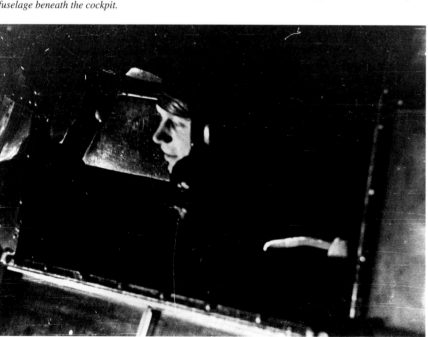

Oblt. Reese of I/NJG 1 just before taking off on a night sortie.

Drawings made by a Feldwebel of I/NJG 3. The drawings depicted life in a night-fighter unit and gave the airmen something to smile about – a rarity in those days. The drawing illustrated in the photo at top right refers to a misfortune suffered by Uffz. Bechthold and Uffz. Harder of 14 Staffel of V/LG 1 in their L1+KK on 13/05/40 (Bechthold's logbook: "Crash, overran the airfield.")

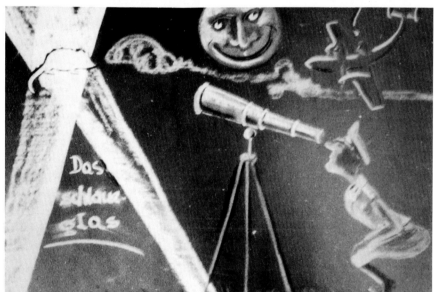
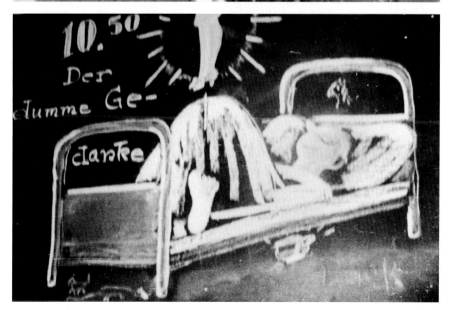

Epilogue

Logically, this history of V (*Zerstörer*) *Gruppe*, *Lehrgeschwader* 1 should be followed by an account of its successor *Gruppe*, I *Gruppe* of *Nachtjagdgeschwader* 3. However the developments that followed until the end of the war became increasingly more complicated. *Staffeln* were transferred to other units, as were *Gruppen*, and later returned to their original units. Surviving log books reveal that crews or parts of them back with the same *Staffel* or *Gruppe* at the end of the war.

Concerning I/NJG 3, the following appears in *Units of the Luftwaffe 1939-1945* by Wolfgang Dierich:

"A Gruppe with the *Geschwader* designation had existed since 1 October 1940, namely I/NJG 3. This was the renamed V/(Z)LG 1, one of the oldest *Zerstörer* and now oldest night-fighter Gruppen in the Luftwaffe. Bases were Vechta, Oldenburg and Wittmundhafen. NJG 3 was under the command of 2nd *Jagddivision*, with the *Geschwaderstab* at Stade and I *Gruppe* based at the airfields in Wunstorf, Vechta and Wittmundhafen. Elements of this *Gruppe* also operated from Rheine and Oldenburg. In spring 1944 the *Geschwaderstab* was based at Stade, I *Gruppe* at Vechta. Toward the end of 1944 the *Geschwader* was at its old bases, with I *Gruppe* at Stade. When the surrender came the *Geschwader* was in the area of Denmark and Schleswig-Holstein."

Paul Zorner (ultimate rank *Major*, *Staffelführer* of 2/NJG 3 until 6 December 1942, *Staffelkapitän* of 3/NJG 3 until September 1943, as of 13 October 1944 *Gruppenkommandeur* of II/NJG 100) wrote in 1991:

"Regarding the copies from *Units of the Luftwaffe 1935 to 1945*, 1st Edition from 1976: Perhaps some corrections have been made in the meantime, but there are still a large number of inaccuracies here. Concerning NJG 3: I was a member of this *Geschwader* from 6/10/42 until 4/4/44. The Stab of I *Gruppe* was based at Vechta this entire time. On 6/12/42 I came from Grove to Wittmundhafen to take over 2/NJG 3 from Hptm. Schönert, and on 16/3/43 I handed it over to Hptm. Becker, who also came from Grove where he was the technical officer. I myself took over 3/NJG 3 at Vechta, however I no longer remember from whom. The *Gruppenkommandeur* was Hptm. Prinz zu Lippe-Weißenfels from Salzburg, with whom I am sure you are familiar. In command of 1 *Staffel* was Oblt. Sosna, another Austrian. From 12 June until the end of July I took part in the then standard 'traveling life' of the experienced night-fighter crews. Then on 25 July 3/NJG 3 was transferred to Wunstorf, then on 8 August to Kastrup. I left the *Staffel* there on 10 September and took over 8/NJG 3 (a unit of III/NJG 3) at Lüneburg."

These are just the opinions of two contributors as an addendum. Perhaps a history of I *Gruppe* of *Nachtjagdgeschwader* 3 (I/NJG 3) will follow.

Appendices

APPENDIX 1
V./(Z) LG 1
List of Flight Personnel 1940

Legend: KIA = Killed in action; WIA = Wounded in action; DCD = Discharged; TFD = Transferred; POW = Prisoner of war; MIA = Missing in action.

14	PT	Lt.	ADAMETZ Hugo	KIA	15/09/1940
15	RO	Uffz.	ARNDT Heinz	KIA	02/04/1940
15	RO	Uffz.	ARNDT Willfried	WIA	17/08/1943
15	PT	Lt.	ALTENDORF Rudolf	DCD	00/00/1945
13	PT	Lt.	BECK Günter	KIA	13/08/1940
13	PT	Lt.	BEYER Franz	TFD	01/04/1940
13	PT	Fw.	BRUNS Adolf	KIA	27/09/1940
13	RO	Uffz.	BUSCH Paul	WIA	08/08/1940
14	PT	Hptm.	BOLTENSTERN v. Hans	TFD	26/08/1940
14	PT	Uffz.	BECHTHOLD Hans	POW	27/09/1940
14	PT	Lt.	BECKER Ludwig	TFD	01/07/1940
14	PT	Lt.	BRAUKMEIER Hans	KIA	04/09/1940
14	RO	Uffz.	BREMSER Karl	KIA	04/09/1940
14	RO	Fw.	BRUNNER Helmut	KIA	08/08/1940
14	PT	Lt.	BONIN v. Eckart	WIA	22/06/1943
15	RO	Uffz.	BANSER Wilhelm	WIA	04/09/1940
15	B F	Uffz.	BRÜGGOW Horst	POW	27/09/1940
15	RO	Uffz.	BUGRAM Gerhard	TFD	30/06/194U
15	PT	Lt.	BUSCHING Hans	KIA	02/04/1940
13	RO	Gcfr.	CONRAD Georg	KIA	12/05/1940
15	PT	Olt.	CLAUSEN Walter	KIA	22/04/1940
13	PT	Fw.	DATZ Hans	POW	13/08/1940
13	RO	Uffz.	DIECKMANN Alfred	WIA	08/08/1940
13	RO	Uffz.	DIERKES Alois	WIA	12/05/1940
14	RO	Ogefr.	DÖPFER Karl	POW	31/08/1940
15	RO	Uffz	DANNERT Johann	TFD	30/05/1940
14	PT	Lt.	EICHHORN Karl	POW	31/08/1940
15	PT	Lt.	EISELE Hermann	KIA	13/07/1940
14	RO	Uffz.	FABIAN Willi	KIA	11/05/1940
14	PT	Olt.	FENSKE Walter	TFD	21/07/1940
14	RO	Uffz.	FRIEDERICH Hans	DCD	00/00/1945
14	PT	Fw.	FRITZ Gottlob	POW	31/08/1940
15	RO	Gefr.	FRESSEL Walter	TFD	18/08/1940
13	PT	Lt.	GAFFAL Hans	WIA	12/05/1940
13	RO	Uffz.	GERIGK Walter	KIA	15/09/1940
13	PT	Olt	GLIENKE Joachim	KIA	25/08/1940
13	PT	Lt.	GOETZE Karl	KIA	11/01/1944
13	PT	Lt.	GORISCH Ernst	KIA	15/09/1940
13	RO	Gefr.	GRÖBL Franz	KIA	27/09/1940
15	RO	Ogefr.	GIGLHUBER Otto	POW	13/08/1940
14	RO	Ogefr.	GROSSE Herbert	WIA	25/08/1940
14	RO	Uffz.	GROWE Richard	KIA	31/08/1940
15	PT	Oblt.	GRAVENREUTH v. Ulrich	KIA	27/09/1940
15	PT	Lt.	GROTEN Josef	TFD	20,03.1940
Stab	PT	Oblt.	GRABMANN Walter	TFD	16/04/1940
13	PT	Uffz.	HARTENSTEIN Kurt	KIA	15/09/1940
13	RO	Uffz.	HOYER Karl	KIA	13/08/1940
14	RO	Gefr.	HAAS Alfred	WIA	13/08/1940
14	RO	Uffz.	HARDER Wilhelm	KIA	21/07/1940
14	RO	Obgefr.	HÜBNER Artur	KIA	27/09/1940
15	PT	Uffz.	HAMANN Horst	KIA	25/08/1940
15	RO	Uffz.	HEIDRICH Erich	TFD	18/11/1940
15	RO	Uffz.	HELDT Paul	TFD	13/08/1940
15	PT	Lt.	HESSEL Ernst	TFD	18/11/1940
13	PT	Fw.	JENTZSCH Gerhard	KIA	08/08/1940
14	RO	Uffz.	JÄCKEL Joachim	POW	04/09/1940
14	PT	Fw.	JECKE Gerhard	WIA	15/08/1940
14	RO	UPTz.	JOHRDEN Friedrich	WIA	22/06/1940
14	PT	Oblt.	JUNGE Michel	KIA	04/09/1940
15	PT	Fw.	JÄCKEL Martin	KIA	01/09/1940
13	PT	Fw.	KINZLER Klaus	KIA	04/01//1940
13	PT	OROw.	KOBERT Rudolf	POW	01/09/1940
Stab	RO	Fw.	KRONE Richard	TFD	16/04/1940
13	RO	Uffz.	KOHRT Fritz	DCD	00/00/1940
14	RO	Uffz.	KOCH Hans	KIA	27/09/1940
14	PT	Lt.	KREBITZ Kurt	WIA	13/07/1940
13	PT	Fw.	KLEVER Georg	WIA	13/08/1940
15	RO	Uffz.	KRAMP Otto	KIA	09/09/1940
14	RO	Obgefr.	KRISCHEWSKI Josef	KIA	14/09/1940
14	RO	Gefr.	KLEMM Fritz	KIA	13/08/1940
Stab	RO	Uffz.	KÖPGE Albert	KIA	27/09/1940
13	BF	Uffz.	LÄMMEL Georg	KIA	13/08/1940

13	BF	Uffz.	LISCHNEWSKI Bruno	WIA	16/12/1940		13	RO	Uffz.	SEUFERT Rudolf	DCD	00/00/1945
14	PT	Lt.	LEICKHARDT Hans	WIA	11/05/1940		13	RO	Uffz.	SOLLUCH Georg	KIA	21/05/1940
14	PT	Fw.	LINDEMANN Friedrich	KIA	27/09/1940		13	PT	Obfw.	STEGEMANN Alois	KIA	21/05/1940
15	RO	Uffz.	LOCHOW Kurt	KIA	13/07/1940		13	RO	Uffz.	STUCK Paul	KIA	25/08/1940
Stab	PT	Hptm.	LIENSBERGER Horst	KIA	27/09/1940		13	FF	Gefr.	SWIETLIK Hans	KIA	27/09/1940
13	RO	Fw.	MEINIG Werner	POW	01/09/1940		14	RO	Obgefr.	SCHMERGAL Karl	WIA	1508/1940
13	RO	Obgefr.	MÖLLER Paul	KIA	04/01/1940		14	RO	Obgefr.	SCHMIDT Heinz	KIA	17/05/1940
13	RO	Uffz.	LANDROCK Willi	KIA	04/01//1940		14	PT	Uffz.	SCHMITT Friedrich	KIA	17/05/1940
13	PT	Lt.	MÜLLER Helmut	KIA	15/09/1940		14	RO	Fw.	SCHNEIDER Fritz	TFD	26/08/1940
14	PT	Hptm.	MAUKE Alexander	SICK	08/08/1940		14	RO	Uffz.	SCHWARZ Kurt	KIA	29/07/1942
14	PT	Oblt.	METHFESSLL Werner	KIA	17/05/1940		14	RO	Uffz.	STEINER Alfred	TFD	21/07/1940
Stab	PT	Oblt.	MÜNTEFERING Franz	TFD	15/07/1940		14	PT	Uffz.	STÖBER Rudolf	DCD	00/00/1945
14	RO	Uffz.	MEINHARD Helmut	TFD	01/07/1940		14	RO	Ogefr.	STIEF Rudolf	KIA	15/09/1940
15	RO	Uffz.	MARESCH Wenzel	KIA	25/08/1940		14	PT	Fw.	STURM Alfred	KIA	08/08/1940
14	PT	Uffz.	NISIEWICZ Hans	TFD	15/09/1940		15	PT	Oblt.	SCHNOOR Emil	TFD	07/08/1940
15	PT	Uffz.	NEUMANN Wilhelm	KIA	04/09/1940		15	PT	Uffz.	SCHÜMICHEN Werner	POW	13/08/1940
13	RO	Uffz.	PAPE Heino	KIA	18/03/1940		15	PT	Lt.	SCHWARZER Georg	KIA	16/05/1940
13	RO	Uffz.	PETRY Willi	KIA	26/03/1940		15	RO	Uffz.	SPEIER Walter	KIA	04/09/1940
13	PT	Hptm.	PETERS Hellmut	DCD	00/00/1940		15	BF	Uffz.	STIER Alfred	TFD	18/08/1940o
Stab	RO	Uffz.	PELLNAT Robert	WIA	16/10/1940		Stab	RO	Uffz.	STECKEMETZ Hans	TFD	16/04/1940
15	RO	Obgefr.	PETRICH Fritz	KIA	16/05/1940		Stab	PT	Oblt.	THIMMIG Wolfgang	TFD	16/04/1940
15	RO	Uffz.	PFAFFELHUBER Alois	KIA	09/09/1940		14	PT	Uffz.	VOELSKOW Peter	WIA	29/07/1942
14	RO	Uffz.	RADECK Kurt	KIA	29/03/1940		13	RO	Uffz.	WENIGER Max	KIA	23/03/1941
14	RO	Uffz.	RESENER Heinz	KIA	17/05/1940		13	RO	Gefr.	WELZ Heinz	KIA	27/09/1940
14	RO	Fw	RÖHRING Karl	KIA	04/09/1940		13	PT	Uffz.	WIEBE Gustav	WIA	12/05/1940
15	RO	Fw	REINHOLD Otto	KIA	27/09/1940		15	PT	Obfw.	WAGNER Heinz	KIA	1308/1940
15	PT	Lt.	RISSMANN Robert	TFD	01//04/1940		15	PT	Fw.	WARRELMANN Altred	WIA	11/08/1940
15	RO	Flg.	RÖSLER Heinz	KIA	01//09/1940		15	PT	Oblt.	WECKEISER Otto	POW	27/09/1940
13	PT	Lt.	SCHMIDT Ernst	KIA	09/03/1941		13	RO	Uffz.	WELLER Hugo	WIA	13/08/1940
13	PT	Lt.	SCHMIDT Hans.	DCD	00/00/1945		14	PT	Lt.	WERNER Horst	KIA	13/08/1940
13	PT	Fw.	SCHOB Herbert	TFD	18/03/1940		14	PT	Fw.	WÜRGATSCH Horst	KIA	21/07/1940
13	PT	Lt.	SCHULTZE Helmut	WIA	12/05/1940		Stab	PT	Oblt.	ZOBEL Ernst	WIA	16/10/1940
13	RO	Uffz	SCHÜTTE Albert	DCD	00/00/1945							

APPENDIX 2
V./(Z) LG 1
Missions – Transfers 1940

DATE	TIME	TAKEOFF	LANDING	TRANSFER/ MISSION	LOSSES			
					KIA	WIA	POW	Bf 110
26/**03/40**	10:45-11:50	Mannheim	Mannheim	Verdun				
29/	14:05-15:55	Mannheim	Mannheim	Verdun	1	1		1
02/**04/40**	11:15-13:05	Mannheim	Mannheim	Nancy	2	1		
20/	09:15-10:50	Mannheim	Mannheim	Trier				
10/**05.40**	05:10-06:45	Mannheim	Mannheim	Verdun				
10/	14:40-16:25	Mannheim	Mannheim	Verdun				
10/	17:40-19:25	Mannheim	Mannheim	Verdun				
11/	06:15-08:50	Mannheim	Mannheim	Verdun	1	1		1
12/	07:20-09:20	Mannheim	Mannheim	Verdun	2	4		3
12/	18:05-20:20	Mannhcim	Mannhcim	Verdun				
13/	12:50-14:50	Mannheim	Mannheim	Verdun				
13/	14:10-16:00	Mannheim	Mannheim	Verdun				
13/	19:35-20:40	Mannheim	Wiesbaden	Verdun				
14/	06:45-8:20	Wiesbaden	Wiesbaden	Verdun				
14/	15:00-17:00	Wiesbaden	Wiesbaden	Verdun				
14/	19:30-21:45	Wiesbaden	Wiesbaden	Verdun				
15/	09:15-11:30	Wiesbaden	Wiesbaden	Sedan				
15/	13:20-15:00	Wiesbaden	Wiesbaden	Sedan				
16/	05:20-07:45	Wiesbaden	Wiesbaden	Reims	2	1		
16/	09:10-11:25	Wiesbaden	Wiesbaden	Reims				
16/	13:40-15:50	Wiesbaden	Wiesbaden	Reims				
17/	10:20-13:00	Wiesbaden	Wiesbaden	Reims	4	1		3
17/	18:15-18:35	Wiesbaden	Wengerohr	Transfer				
18/	09:10-11:00	Wengerohr	Wengerohr	Reims				
18/	15:00-16:00	Wengerohr	Neufchateau	Compiegne				
19/	09:20-09:40	Neufchateau	Trier	Transfer				
19/	13:50-15:50	Trier	Trier	Epemay				
20/	05:25-07:30	Trier	Trier	St. Quentin				
20/	10:10-10:30	Trier	St.Made	Transfer				
21/	18:15-20:25	St.Marie	St.Marie	Amiens	2			1
23/	18:40-20:05	St.Marie	St.Made	Amiens				
24/	13:40-15:30	St.Made	St.Made	Amiens				
25/	07:45-9:30	St.Made	St.Made	Beauvais				
25/	14:15-15:50	St.Made	St.Marie	Amiens				
25/	18:30-20:30	St.Marie	St.Made	Amiens				
26/	13:15-14:55	St.Made	St.Made	Lagny				
25/	17:45-20:05	St.Marie	St.Made	Amiens				
27/	12:50-15/15	St.Made	St.Made	Dunkirk				
27/	19:00-21:05	St.Made	St.Made	Dunkirk				
28/	19:00-21:00	St.Made	St.Made	Amiens				
29/	19/00-21:15	St.Made	St.Made	Amiens				
01/**06/40**	16:55-17:45	St.Marie	St.Marie	Adon				
03/	13:20-15:40	St.Ma(ie	St.Made	Paris				
06/	13:55-15:35	St.Made	St.Made	Paris				
07/	05:15-07:15	St.Marie	St.Made	Clermont				
07/	12:55-15:05	St.Marie	St.Made	Clermont				
09/	19:35-21:35	St.Marie	St.Made	Rethel				
10/	12:35-14:20	St.Marie	St.Made	Rethel				
10/	18:25-20:45	St.Made	St.Made	Reims				
11/	18:05-19:10	St.Marie	St.Marie	Rethel				

Zerstörergruppe

DATE	TIME	TAKEOFF	LANDING	TRANSFER/ MISSION	LOSSES			
					KIA	WIA	POW	Bf 110
11/	20:30-21:20	St.Marie	St.Marie	Rethel				
12/	15:40-16:30	St.Marie	St.Marie	Rethel				
14/	15:10-16:50	St.Marie	St.Marie	Toul				
15/	06:00-07:10	St.Marie	St.Marie	Verdun				
15/	14:15-16:15	St.Marie	St.Marie	Verdun				
16/	09:45-11:40	St.Marie	St.Marie	Rethel				
28/	17:10-18:40	St.Marie	La Mans	Transfer				
29/	18:00-18:20	Le Mans	Alencon	Transfer				
03/**07/40**	05:50-06:40	Alencon	Cherbourg	Transfer				
03/	20:45-21:55	Cherbourg	Alencon	Transfer				
04/	05:45-06:30	Alencon	Cherbourg	Transfer				
04/	09:15-10:20	Cherbourg	Cherbourg	Portland				
04/	15:15-16:15	Cherbourg	Cherbourg	Portland				
04/	20:20-21:55	Cherbourg	Alencon	Transfer				
07/	12:45-13:15	Alencon	Cherbourg	Transfer				
07/	17:20-19:00	Cherbourg	Cherbourg	Plymouth				
07/	21:10-21:55	Cherbourg	Alencon	Transfer				
08/	08:00-08:30	Alencon	Cherbourg	Transfer				
08/	09:00-10:35	Cherbourg	Cherbourg	Plymouth				
08/	15:20-17:00	Cherbourg	Cherbourg	Plymouth				
08/	20:05-20:45	Cherbourg	Alencon	Transfer				
09/	13:30-14:10	Alencon	Cherbourg	Transfer				
09/	17:00-18:05	Cherbourg	Cherbourg	Portland				
09/	20:00-21:30	Cherbourg	Cherbourg	Portland				
10/	20:45-21:35	Cherbourg	Alencon	Transfer				
11/	08:40-09:25	Alencon	Cherbourg	Transfer				
11/	12:00-13:30	Cherbourg	Cherbourg	Plymouth				
11/	19:05-20/15	Cherbourg	Alencon	Transfer				
12/	10:00-10:30	Alencon	Rocquancourt	Transfer				
12/	17:30-19:40	Rocquanc	Rocquancourt	Isle of Wight				
13/	05:40-06:10	Rocquanc	Cherbourg	Transfer				
13/	08:20-09:10	Cherbourg	Cherbourg	Isle of Wight				
13/	15:40-17:00	Cherbourg	Cherbourg	Isle of Wight	2	1		1
13/	18:25-18:50	Cherbourg	Rocquancourt	Transfer				
14/	06:45-07:15	Rocquanc	Theville	Transfer				
14/	08:30-09:30	Theville	Theville	Portland				
14/	11:20-12:40	Theville	Theville	Portland				
14/	15:25-16:55	Theville	Theville	Portland				
14/	18:15-18:50	Theville	Rocquancourt	Transfer				
21/	09:40-11:05	Rocquanc	Rocquancourt	Isle of Wight				
21/	12:50-13:20	Rocquanc	Theville	Transfer				
21/	15:50-17:15	Theville	Theville	Isle of Wight	2			1
21/	19:50-20:45	Theville	Theville	Isle of Wight				
21/	21:45-22:15	Theville	Rocquancourt	Transfer				
22/	13:05-14:15	Rocquanc	Rocquancourt	Isle of Wight				
26/	13:15-13:40	Rocquanc	Cherbourg	Transfer				
26/	15:35-16:25	Cherbourg	Cherbourg	Isle of Wight				
26/	19:40-20:50	Cherbourg	Cherbourg	Isle of Wight				
26/	21:25-21:50	Cherbourg	Rocquancourt	Transfer				
04/**08/40**	16:00-17:05	Rocquanc	Rocquancourt	Isle of Wight				
08/	09:25-10:45	Rocquanc	Rocquancourt	Isle of Wight				
08/	12:00-12:25	Rocquanc	Cherbourg	Transfer				
08/	12:50-14:10	Cherbourg	Cherbourg	Isle of Wight	3	2		2
08/	16:35-17:50	Cherbourg	Cherbourg	Isle of Wight				
08/	19:15-19:40	Cherbourg	Rocquancourt	Transfer				

DATE	TIME	TAKEOFF	LANDING	TRANSFER/ MISSION	LOSSES			
					KIA	WIA	POW	Bf 110
11/	08:15-08:45	Rocquanc	Lessay	Transfer				
11/	10:40-12:10	Lessay	Rocquancourt	Portland				
12/	09:25-09:50	Rocquanc	Lessay	Transfer				
12/	12:10-14:10	Lessay	Rocquancourt	Portsmouth				
13/	06:40-08:10	Rocquanc	Rocquancourt	Brighton				
13/	12:10-14:10	Rocquanc	Rocquancourt	Borunem	7	4	3	5
15/	14:30-14:50	Rocquanc	Lessay	Transfer				
15/	17:25-19:30	Lessay	Rocquancourt	Portland				
16/	13:25-15:00	Rocquanc	Rocquancourt	Portsmouth				
16/	17:30-19:45	Rocquanc	Rocquancourt	Aldershot				
20/	14:00-14:20	Rocquanc	Lessay	Transfer				
20/	17:10-17:45	Lessay	Rocquancourt	Transfer				
23/	09:15-09:35	Rocquanc	Lessay	Transfer				
23/	16:20-17:10	Lessay	Rocquancourt	Transfer				
24/	16:45-18:15	Rocquanc	Rocquancourt	Isle of Wight				
25/	12:35-12:55	Rocquanc	Lessay	Transfer				
25/	17:20-19:20	Lessay	Rocquancourt	Portland	4	1		2
26/	16:30-18:30	Rocquanc	Rocquancourt	Portsmouth				
28/	16:15-16:50	Rocquanc	Ligescourt	Transfer				
29/	15:50-17:45	Ligescourt	Ligescourt	London				
30/	11-//00-12:50	Ligescourt	Ligescourt	London				
30/	16:50-18:20	Ligescourt	Ligescourt	London				
31/	08:35-10:55	Ligescourt	Ligescourt	London	1	3		2
01/**09/40**	14:00-15:50	Ligescourt	Ligescourt	London	2	2		2
02/	16:30-18:20	Ligescourt	Ligescourt	London				
04/	13:30-15:15	Ligescourt	Ligescourt	London	7	1	1	4
06/	09:00-10:50	Ligescourt	Ligescourt	London				
07/	17:45-19:35	Ligescourt	Ligescourt	London				
08/	12:30-14:10	Ligescourt	Ligescourt	London				
09/	17:45-19:35	Ligescourt	Ligescourt	London	2		1	
11/	12:55-13:55	Ligescourt	Cherbourg	Transfer				
11/	16:00-17:50	Cherbourg	Cherbourg	Southampton				
11/	18:10-19:05	Cherbourg	Ligescourt	Transfer				
15/	14:35-16:25	Ligescourt	Ligescourt	London	6		3	
16/	08:15-09:35	Ligescourt	Ligescourt	London				
27/	09:35-11:45	Ligescourt	Ligescourt	London	11		3	7
05/**10/40**	11:20-11:50	Ligescourt	Brussels	Transfer				
05/	14:35-15:10	Brussels	Cologne	Transfer				
10/	16:10-17:30	Cologne	Ingolstadt	Transfer				
16/	14:40-16:05	Ingolstadt	Memmingen	Transfer				
20/	15:30-16:20	Memmingen	Stuttgart	Transfer				

APPENDIX 3
Missions by V./(Z) LG 1

September 1939

01:	10:15	Escort, Warsaw, air combat
01:	16:15	Escort, Warsaw
03:	06:50	Escort, Warsaw, air combat
03:	17:10	Free chase, Ploch, flak, air combat, radio operator Uffz. Rahlfs/13 St., pilot Uffz. Mazurowski-radio operator Uffz. Lothar, pilot Uffz. Plankenhorn-radio operator Gefr. Kottmann/15 St. KIA
04:	09:35	Low-level attacks on rail lines, Warsaw
04:	15:55	Escort, low-level attacks, Warsaw, flak
05:	16:45	Free chase, Warsaw, air combat
06:	09:35	Low-level attacks on rail lines, Bialystok, flak
06:	16:40	Escort, Bialystok
07:	15:40	Escort, Deblin, flak, pilot Hptm. Schleif, radio operator Uffz. Haupp/15 St. KIA
08:	09:15	Free chase, Warsaw
08:	15-05	Escort, Warsaw, flak
09:	09:35	Escort, Warsaw
09:	11:45	Escort, Radzyn
09:	17:00	Escort, Siedlce
10:	10:20	Escort, Modlin-Warsaw, flak
10:	13:50	Low-level attacks on rail lines, Warsaw
11:	09-10	Free chase, Wyskow-Minsk
15:	13:45	Low-level attacks, Baranowicze-Slonim
17:	10-.45	Low-level attacks, Gabin

October 1939

04:	11:20	Border patrol, Prmasens-Trier-Wiesbaden
04:	15:50	Border patrol
13:	15:40	Border patrol
14:	15:40	Border patrol
16:	11:15	Border patrol
16:	15:30	Border patrol
19:	11:30	Border patrol
30:	13:40	Border patrol, Bitburg-Morzig

January 1940

04:	11:30	Air combat practise, pilot Fw. Kinzler-radio operator Uffz. Landrock, radio operator Obgefr. Möller/13 St. fatally injured.

March 1940

26:	10:45	Escort for reconnaissance aircraft, Verdun. Air combat, forced landings: pilot Fw. Datz/13 St. near Lutzerath, Uffz. Warrelmann/15 St. near Mainz
29:	14:05	Border patrol, air combat, pilot Fw, Lindemann-radio operator Uffz. Radeck/14 St.shot down, Uffz. Radeck killed.

April 1940

02:	11:13	Escort for reconnaissance aircraft, Nancy, air combat, pilot Lt. Busching-radio operator Uffz. Amdt/15 St. killed
20:	9:15	Border patrol, Saarbrücken-Trier

May 1940

10:	05:07	Escort, Metz-Verdun,flak
10:	14:10	Escort, Sedan-Verdun,flak
10:	17:40	Escort, Neufchateau
11:	06:15	Escort, Sedan-Verdun,flak, Air combat, pilot Lt. Leickhardt-radio operator Uffz. Fabian/14 St. shot down, Lt. Leickhardt injured, POW, Uffz. Fabian killed

12:	7:00	Escort, Sedan-Mourmelon, flak, air combat, pilot Uffz. Hartenstein-radio operator Uffz. Conrad/13 St. killed, pilot Lt. Schultze-radio operator Uffz. Wiebe/13 St. POW, pilot Lt. Gaffal-radio operator Uffz. Dierkes/13 St. POW
12:	18:00	Escort, Sedan-Charleville, flak, air combat
13:	19:34	Escort, Sedan
14:	06:44	Escort for reconnaissance aircraft, Sedan-Verdun,-flak
14:	14:55	Escort, Sedan-Verdun, flak
14:	19:30	Free chase, Sedan-Verdun
15:	09:16	Escort, Sedan, flak
15:	13:20	Escort, Charleville, flak
16:	05:20	Escort, Rethel-Reims, flak, air combat, pilot Lt. Schwarzer-radio operator Ogefr. Petrich/l 5 St. killed
16:	09:09	Escort, Reims, flak
16:	13:40	Escort, Reims, flak
17:	10:20	Escort, Reims-Metz, flak, air combat pilot Oblt.Methfessel-radio operator Uffz. Resener/14 St. killed, pilot Uffz. Schmitt-radio operator Ogefr. Schmidt/14St. killed,
18:	09:12	Escort, Reims-Charleville
18:	15:00	Escort, Amiens-Abbeville
19:	13:30	Escort, Epernay-Compiegne, flak, air combat
20:	05:25	Escort, Moutidier-Soissons,flak, air combat
21:	18:00	Escort, Amiens-Pontoise, flak, air combat, pilot Obfw. Stegemann-radio operator Uffz. Solluch/l3 St. killed in takeoff crash.
23:	18:40	Escort, Arras-Cambrai
24:	13:30	Escort, Beauvais-Amiens, air combat
25:	07:45	Escort, Beauvais-Amiens, air combat
25:	13:50	Escort, Amiens-St-Quentin, flak, air combat
25:	18:30	Escort, Amiens-St.Quentin, air combat
26:	17:45	Escort, Arras-Le Havre
26:	13:15	Escort, Paris, flak
27:	12:50	Escort, Dunkirk, air combat
27:	19:00	Escort, Dunkirk, air combat
28:	19:00	Escort, Amiens, flak
29:	19:00	Escort, Amiens, flak

June 1940

0l:	16:55	Escort for reconnaissance aircraft, Arlon, flak
03:	13:20	Escort, Paris, flak
06:	13:50	Escort, Reims-Paris, flak
07:	05:15	Escort, Clermont, flak
07:	12:50	Escort, Clermont, flak
09:	19:30	Escort, Rethel, flak
10:	12:35	Escort, Rethel-Vouziers, flak
10:	18:25	Escort, Rethei-Eperney, flak
11:	18:05	Escort, Epemey-Chadons
12:	20:25	Escort, Rethel-Reims, flak
12:	15:40	Escort, Rethel-Revigny, flak
14:	15:10	Escort, Epinal-Toul, flak
15:	0600	Escort, Verdun-Vesoul, flak
15:	1415	Escort, Verdun-Toul, flak
16:	09:45	Escort, Rethel

July 1940

04:	09:05	Escort for Stukas, Portland-Weymouth, convoy, flak
04:	14:15	Escort for Stukas, Channel, convoy, flak
07:	17:20	Escort for reconnaissance aircraft, Portland-Plymouth
08:	15:20	Escort, for reconnaissance aircraft, Portland-Plymouth
08:	09:00	Escort for reconnaissance aircraft, Portland-Plymouth
09:	17:00	Escort for Stukas, Channel, picket boat
09:	19:50	Escort for Stukas, Portland, air combat, pilot Oblt. Glienke-radio operator Uffz. Hoyer/13 St. shot down, rescued by He 59

09:	21:40	Search for Oblt. Glienke-Uffz. Hoyer
1l:	11:55	Escort for Stukas, Weymouth
12:	17:30	Escort for reconnaissance aircraft, Isle of Wight, air combat
13:	08:20	Escort for reconnaissance aircraft, Isle of Wight
13:	15:38	Escort for reconnaissance aircraft, Portland, flak, air combat, pilot Lt. Eisele-radio operator Uffz. Lochow/ 15 St. killed, pilot Lt. Krebitz/14 St. wounded
14:	08:30	Escort for reconnaissance aircraft, Isle of Wight
14:	10:30	Escort for Stukas, Isle of Wight
14:	15:25	Reconnaissance of British early-warning system, Channel coast
21:	09:40	Escort for reconnaissance aircraft, Isle of Wight, air combat
21:	15:50	Escort for Stukas, Isle of Wight, convoy, air combat, pilot Fw. Würgatsch-radio operator Uffz. Harder/14 St. killed in crash landing near Cherbourg
21:	19:50	Escort, Isle of Wight, convoy
22:	13:05	Escort for reconnaissance aircraft, Isle of Wight
26:	15:35	Escort, Isle of Wight
26:	19:40	Escort for Stukas, Portland

August 1940

04:	16:00	Channel reconnaissance
08:	09:25	Escort for Stukas, Isle of Wight
08:	12:50	Escort fair Stukas, Isle of Wight, convoy, air combat, pilot Fw. Sturm-radio operator Fw. Brunner/14 St. killed, radio operator Uffz. Busch/13 St. wounded, crash landing by pilot Fw. Jentzsch-radio operator Uffz. Dieckmann/13 St. at Cherbourg, Fw. Jentzsch killed, Uffz. Dieckmann wounded
08:	16:40	Escort for Stukas, Isle of Wight, convoy, air combat
1l:	10:40	Escort, Isle of Wight, flak
12:	12:10	Escort, Isle of Wight-Portsmouth, flak, air combat
13:	06:40	Escort, Brighton-Guildford, air combat
13:	12:10	Escort, Bournemouth, air combat, killed: pilot Lt. Beck-radio operator Uffz. Hoyer/13 St., pilot Lt. Werner-radio operator Gefr.Klemm/14 St., pilot Obfw. Wagner-radio operator Uffz. Heldt/15 St radio operator Uffz. Lämmel/13 St.,POW: pilot Fw. Datz/13 St., pilot Uffz. Schümichen-radio operator Ogefr. Giglhuber/ 15 St., Wounded: pilot Fw. Klever-radio operator Uffz. Weller/13 St., radio operator Gefr. Haas/14 St., pilot Fw. Jecke/14 St.
15:	17:25	Escort, Portland, air combat
16:	13:20	Escort, Portsmouth
16:	17:30	Escort, London
24:	16:40	Escort, Isle of Wight
25:	17:20	Escort for Stukas, Portland, flak, air combat, killed: pilot Oblt. Glienke-radio operator Uffz. Stuck/13St., pilot Uffz. Hamann-radio operator Uffz. Maresch/15 St., wounded: radio operator Ogefr. Große/14 St.
26:	16:30	Escort, Portsmouth, flak
29:	15:50	Free chase, London
30:	11:00	Escort, London, air combat
31:	08:30	Escort, north of London, air combat, killed: radio operator Uffz. Growe/14 St.,POW: pilot Lt. Eichhom/ 14 St., pilot Fw. Fritz-radio operator Ogefr. Döpfer/14 St.

September 1940

01:	14:00	Escort, London, flak, air combat, pilot Fw. Jägel-radio operator Flg. Rösler/15 St. killed, POW; pilot Obfw. Kobert-radio operator Fw. Meinig/13 St.
02:	16:20	Escort, London, flak, air combat
04:	13:25	Escort for Bf 110 bombers, Aldershot, flak, air combat; killed: pilot Oblt. Junge-radio operator Fw. Bremser/ 14 St., pilot Lt. Braukmeier-radio operator Ogefr. Krischweski/14 St., pilot Fw. Röhring/14 St. pilot Uffz. Neumann-radio operator Uffz. Speier/15 St. (crash landing near Boulogne); POW: radio operator Uffz. Jäckel/14 St.; wounded: radio operator Uffz. Banser/15 St.
06:	09:00	Free chase, London, flak
07:	17:45	Escort, London, flak
08:	12:30	Escort, London
09:	17:45	Free chase, London, flak, air combat, pilot Uffz. Pfaffelhuber-radio operator Uffz. Kramp/15 St. killed
1l:	16:00	Escort for Bf 110 bombers, Southampton, air combat
15:	14:35	Escort, London, air combat; killed: Pilot Oblt. Müller-radio operator Fw. Hoffmann/13 St., pilot Lt. Gorisch-radio operator Uffz. Gerigk/13 St., pilot Lt. Adametz-radio operator Ogefr. Stief/14 St.

16:     08:15   Free chase, London, flak
27:     09:30   Escort, flak, air combat. Killed: pilot Fw. Bruns-radio operator Gefr. Göbl/13 St., pilot Gefr. Swietlik-radio operator Gefr. Weiz/13 St., pilot Fw. Lindemann-radio operator Ogefr. Hübner/14 St., radio operator Uffz. Koch/14 St., pilot Oblt. v. Gravenreuth-radio operator FW Reinhold/15 St., pilot Hptm. Liensberger-radio operator Uffz. Köpge/Stab; POW: pilot Uffz. Bechthold/14 St., pilot Oblt. Weckeiser-radio operator Uffz. Brüggow/15 St.

APPENDIX 4
Casualties
V./(Z) LG 1
1939

Summer 1939: I/(schw.Jagd) LG 1 renamed V/(Zerstörer) LG 1
Former 1, 2 and 3 Staffeln became 13, 14 and 15 Staffeln

13 Staffel:

PILOT	Fw.	DATZ Hans	
RO	Uffz.	LAMMEL Georg	
PILOT	Lt.	GAFFAL Hans	
RO	Uffz.	PETRY Willi	
PILOT	Fw.	KINZLER,Willi	
RO	Obgefr.	MÖLLER Paul	
PILOT	Oblt.	GLIENKE Joachim	
RO	Uffz.	LANDROCK Willi	
PILOT	Fw.	KOBERT Rudolf	
RO	Fw.	MEINIG Werner	
PILOT	Oblt.	MULLER Helmut (Kap.)	
RO	Uffz.	RAHLFS Walter	KIA 03/09/39
RO	Uffz.	DIERKES Alois	WIA 06/09/39
RO	Fw.	HOFFMANN Andreas	
PILOT	Obfw.	SCHOB Herbert	
RO	Uffz.	PAPE Heino	
PILOT	Obfw.	STEGEMANN Alois	
RO	Uffz.	SOLLUCH Georg	
PILOT	Fw.	STERN Gerhard	KIA 16/12/39
RO	Uffz.	TIETZ Walther	KIA 16/12/39

14 Staffel:

PILOT	Olt.	FENSKE Walter	
RO	Uffz.	STEINER Alfred	
PILOT	Fw.	JECKE Gerhard	
RO	Ogefr.	SCHMERGAL Karl	
PILOT	Fw.	LINDEMANN Friedrich	
RO	Uffz.	RADECK Kurt	
PILOT	Olt.	METHFESSEL Werner (Kap.)	
RO	Uffz.	RESENER Heinz	
PILOT	Fw.	STURM Alfred	
OF	Fw.	BRUNNER Helmut	
PILOT	Lt.	WERNER Horst	
RO	Uffz.	BREMSER Karl	WIA 03.09.39
RO	Uffz.	HARDER Wilhelm	

3 Staffel:

PILOT	Lt.	BUSCHING Hans	
RO	Uffz.	ARNDT Heinz	
PILOT	Olt.	CLAUSEN-.Walter (Kap.)	
RO	Fw.	REINHOLD Otto	
PILOT	Uffz.	GROTEN Josef	
RO	Uffz.	LOCHOW Kurt	

V/(Z)LG 1

13 Staffel

PT	Fw.	BRUNS Adolf	KIA 27/09/40
RO	Gefr.	GRÖBL Franz	KIA 27/09/40
PT	Lt.	BECK Günther	KIA 13/08/40
RO	Uffz.	BUSCH Paul	WIA 08/08/40
RO	Uffz.	HOYER Karl	KIA 13/08/40
PT	Fw.	DATZ Hans	POW 13/08/40
RO	Uffz.	LÄMMEL Georg	KIA 13/08/40
PT	Lt.	GAFFAL Hans	WIA 12/05/40
RO	Uffz.	PETRY Willi	KIA 26/03/40
RO	Uffz.	DIERKES Alois	WIA 12/05/40
PT	Oblt.	GLIENKE Joachim	KIA 25/08/40
RO	Uffz.	LANDROCK Willi	KIA 04/01/40
RO	Uffz.	HOYER Karl	WIA 09/07/40
RO	Uffz.	STUCK Paul	KIA 25/08/40
PT	Lt.	GORISCH Ernst	KIA 15/09/40
RO	Uffz.	GERIGK Walter	KIA 15/09/40
PT	Lt.	GOETZE Karl	KIA 10/01/44
RO	Uffz.	SEUFERT Rudolf	DCD 00/00/45
PT	Uffz.	HARTENSTEIN Kurt	KIA 12/05/40
RO	Gefr.	CONRAD Georg	KIA 12/05/40
PT	Fw.	JENTZSCH Gerhard	KIA 08/08/40
RO	Uffz.	DIECKMARN Alfred	WIA 08/08/40
PT	Fw.	KLEVER Georg	KIA 03/04/45
RO	Uffz.	WELLER Hugo	WIA 13/08/40
RO	Uffz.	WIEBE Gustav	DCD 00/00/45

PT	Fw.	KINZLER Willi	KIA 04/01/40
RO	Obgefr.	MÖLLER Paul	KIA 04/01/40
PT	Obfw.	KOBERT Rudolf	POW 01/09/40
RO	Fw.	MEINIG Werner	POW 01/09/40
PT	Oblt.	MÜLLER Helmut (Kap.)	KIA 15/09/40
RO	Fw.	HOFFMANN Andreas	KIA 15/09/40
PT	Hptm.	PETERS Hellmut (Kap.)	DCD 00/00/45
RO	Uffz.	KOHRT Fritz	DCD 00/00/45
PT	Lt.	SCHMIDT Ernst	KIA 23/03/41
RO	Uffz.	WENIGER Max	KIA 23/03/41
PT	Lt.	SCHMIDT Hans	DCD 00/00/45
RO	Uffz.	SCHÜTTE Albert	DCD 00/00/45
PT	Obfw.	SCHOB Herbert	TFD 18/03/40
RO	Uffz.	PAPE Heino	TFD 18/03/40
PT	Lt.	SCHULTZE	WIA 12/05/40
RO	Uffz.	WIEBE Gustav	WIA 12/05/40
PT	Obfw.	STEGEMANN Alois	KIA 21/05/40
RO	Uffz.	SOLLUCH Georg	KIA 21/05/40
PT	Gefr.	SWIETLIK Hans	KIA 27/09/40
RO	Gefr.	WELZ Heinz	KIA 27/09/40

14 Staffel

PT	Lt.	ADAMETZ Hugo	KIA 15/09/40
RO	Obgefr.	STIEF Rudolf	KIA 15/09/40
PT	Uffz.	BECHTHOLD Hans	POW 27/09/40
RO	Uffz.	KOCH Hans	KIA 27/09/40
PT	Lt.	BECKER Ludwig	TFD 01/07/40
RO	Uffz.	MEINHARD Helmut	DCD 00/00/45
PT	Hptm.	BOLTENSTERN v. Hans (Kap.)	TFD 26/06/40
RO	Fw.	SCHNEIDER Fritz	TFD 26/08/40
PT	Lt.	BONIN v. Eckert	WIA 22/06/43
RO	Uffz.	JOHRDEN Friedrich	WIA 22/06/43
PT	Lt.	BRAUKMEIER Hans	KIA 04/09/40
RO	Ogefr.	KRISCHEWSKI Josef	KIA 04/09/40
PT	Lt.	EICHHORN Karl	POW 31/08/40
R O	Uffz.	GROWE Richard	KIA 31/08/40
PT	Oblt.	FENSKE Walter	TFD 21/07/40
RO	Uffz.	STEINER Alfred	TFD 21/07/40
PT	Fw.	FRITZ Gottlob	POW 31/08/40
RO	Obgefr.	DÖPFER Karl	POW 31/08/40
PT	Fw.	JECKE Gerhard	WIA 15/08/40
RO	Obgefr.	SCHMERGAL Karl	WIA 15/08/40
PT	Oblt.	JUNGE Michel (Kap.)	KIA 04/09/40
RO	Gefr.	HAAS Alfred	WIA 13/08/40
BF	Fw.	BREMSER Karl	KIA 04/09/40
PT	Lt.	KREBITZ Kurt	WIA 13/07/40
RO	Uffz.	KOCH Hans	KIA 27/09/40
PT	Lt.	LEICKHARDT Hans	WIA 12/05/40

RO	Uffz.	FABIAN Willi	KIA 12/05/40
PT	Fw.	LINDEMANN Friedrich	KIA 27/09/40
RO	Uffz.	RADECK Kurt	KIA 29/03/40
RO	Obgefr.	HÜBNER Artur	KIA 27/09/40
PT	Hptm.	MAUKE Alexander (Kap.)	SICK 08/08/40
RO	Uffz.	KOCH Hans	KIA 27/09/40
PT	Oblt.	METHFESSEL Werner (Kap.)	KIA 17/05/40
RO	Uffz.	RESENER Heinz	KIA 17/05/40
PT	Uffz.	NISIEWICZ Hans	TFD 15/09/40
RO	Uffz.	JÄCKEL Joachim	POW 04/09/40
PT	Fw.	RÖHRING Karl	KIA 04/09/40
RO	Obgefr.	GROSSE Herbert	WIA 25/08/40
RO	Uffz.	JÄCKEL Joachim	POW 04/09/40
PT	Lt.	SCHALKHAUSSER Kurt	WIA 17/05/40
RO	Uffz.	JÄCKEL Joachim	WIA 17/05/40
PT	Uffz.	SCHMITT Friedrich	KIA 17/05/40
RO	Obgefr.	SCHMIDT Heinz	KIA 17/05/40
PT	Fw.	STURM Alfred	KIA OB.08/40
RO	Fw.	BRUNNER Helmut	KIA 06/08/40
PT	Uffz.	VOELSKOW Peter	WIA 29/07/42
RO	Uffz.	SCHWARZ Kurt	KIA 29/07/42
PT	Lt.	WERNER Horst	KIA 13/08/40
RO	Gefr.	KLEMM Fritz	KIA 13/08/40
PT	Fw.	WÜRGATSCH Horst	KIA 21/07/40
RO	Uffz.	HARDER Willi	KIA 21/07/40
PT	Uffz.	STOBER Rudolf	DCD 00/00/45
RO	Uffz.	FRIEDERICH Hans	DCD 00/00/45

15 Staffel

PT	Lt.	ALTENDORF Rudolf	DCD 00/00/45
RO	Uffz.	ARNDT Wilfried	WIA 17/08/43
PT	Lt.	BUSCHING Hans	KIA 02/04/40
RO	Uffz.	ARNDT Heinz	KIA 02/04/40
PT	Oblt.	CLAUSEN Walter (Kap.)	KIA 22/04/40
RO	Fw.	REINHOLD Otto	KIA 27/09/40
PT	Oblt.	GRAVENREUTH v. Ulrich (Kap.)	KIA 27/09/40
RO	Fw.	REINHOLD Otto	KIA 27/09/40
PT	Lt.	EISELE Hermann	KIA 13/07/40
RO	Uffz.	LOCHOW Kurt	KIA 13/07/40
PT	Uffz.	GROTEN Josef	TFD 20/03/40
RO	Uffz.	LOCHOW Kurt	KIA 13/07/40
PT	Lt.	HESSEL Ernst	TFD 18/11/40
RO	Gefr.	FRESSEL Walter	TFD 18/08/40
RO	Uffz.	BUGRAM Gerhard	TFD 30/08/40
RO	Uffz.	HEIDRICH Erich	TFD 18/11/40
PT	Uffz.	HAMANN Horst	KIA 25/08/40
RO	Uffz.	MARESCH Wenzel	KIA 25/08/40
PT	Fw.	JÄCKEL Martin	KIA 01/09/40
RO	Flg.	RÖSLER Heinz	KIA 01/09/40

PT	Uffz.	NEUMANN Wilhelm	KIA 04/09/40
RO	Uffz.	SPEIER Walter	KIA 04/09/40
PT	Uffz.	PFAFFELHUBER Alois	KIA 09/09/40
RO	Uffz.	STIER Alfred	TFD 18/08/40
RO	Uffz.	BANSER Wilhelm	WIA 04/09/40
RO	Uffz.	KRAMP Otto	KIA 09/09/40
PT	Lt.	RISSMANN Robert	TFD 01/04/40
RO	Obgefr.	PETRICH Fritz	KIA 16/05/40
PT	Oblt.	SCHNOOR Emil (Kap.)	TFD 07/08/40
RO	Fw.	REINHOLD Otto	KIA 27/09/40
PT	Uffz.	SCHÜMICHEN Werner	POW 13/06/40
RO	Obgefr.	GIGLHUBER Otto	POW 13/08/40
PT	Lt.	SCHWARZER Georg	KIA 16/05/40
RO	Obgefr.	PETRICH Fritz	KIA 16/05/40
PT	Ofw.	WAGNER Heinz	KIA 13/08/40
RO	Uffz.	HELDT Paul	KIA 13/08/40
PT	Fw.	WARRELMANN Alfred	WIA 11/08/40
RO	Uffz.	KRAMP Otto	KIA 09/09/40
PT	Uffz.	MAZUROWSKI Sigismund	KIA 03/09/39
RO	Uffz.	LOTHAR Günther	KIA 03/09/39
PT	Uffz.	PLANKENHORN Walter	KIA 03/09/39
RO	Gefr.	KOTTMANN Hermann	KIA 03/09/39
PT.	Hptm.	SCHLEIF Fritz (Kap.)	KIA 07/09/39
RO	Uffz.	HAUPP Franz	KIA 07/09/39
PT	Uffz.	SYNDT Hermann	
RO	Uffz.	BRÜGGOW Horst	
PT	Uffz.	WARRELMANN Alfred	
RO	Uffz.	KRAMP Otto	
PT	Lt.	WECKEISER Otto	
RO	Uffz.	BRAHMANN Willi	
PT	Lt.	ZOBEL Ernst	
RO	Uffz.	PELLNAT Robert	
PT	Uffz.	HERMANN Werner	
RO	Gefr.	BOCKMÜHL Otto	
PT	Uffz.	LANGE Willi	
RO	Uffz.	HELDT Paul	

Stab

PT	Obstlt.	GRABMANN Walter (Kommandeur) TFD 16/04/40
RO	Fw.	KRONE Richard TFD 16/04/40
PT	Hptm.	LIENSBERGER Horst (Kommandeur) KIA 27/09/40
RO	Uffz.	KÖPGE Albert KIA 27/09/40
PT	Oblt.	MÜNTEFERING (TO) (Kap./14/St.) TFD 15/07/40
RO	Fw.	SCHNEIDER Fritz TFD 26/08/40
PT	Olt.	THIMMIG Wolfgang (Adjutant) TFD 16/04/40
RO	Uffz.	STECKEMETZ Hans TFD 16/04/40
PT	Olt.	ZOBEL Ernst (Adj.) (Kap./14/St.) WIA 16/10/40
RO	Uffz.	PELLNAT Robert WIA 16/10/40

I/NJG 3
(I Gruppe of Nachtjagdgeschwaders 3)
Crews of the former V./(Z)LG 1 01/1940

1 Staffel:

PT	Fw.	JECKE Gerhard	TFD 01/10/42
RO	Uffz.	SCHMERGAL Karl	TFD 01/10/42
PT	Fw.	KLEVER Georg	TFD 01/02/44
RO	Uffz.	LISCHNEWSKI Bruno	WIA 16/12/43
PT	Hptm.	PETERS Hellmut	TFD 15/10/41
RO	Uffz.	KOHRT Fritz	TFD 15/10/41
PT	Lt.	SCHMIDT Ernst	KIA 23/03/41
RO	Uffz.	WENIGER Max	KIA 23/03/41
PT	Lto	SCHMIDT Hans	TFD 23/03/41
RO	Uffz.	SCHÜTTE Albert	TFD 23/03/41
PT	Lt.	SCHULTZE Helmut	TFD 01/10/42
RO	Uffz.	WIEBE Gustav	TFD 01/10/42
PT	Oblt.	(WEEGMANN v. Horst)	KIA 09/03/41
RO	Uffz.	BANSER Wilhelm	KIA 09/03/41

2 Staffel

PT	Lt.	BONIN v. Eckert	TFD 24/10/40
RO	Uffz.	JOHRDEN Friedrich	TFD 24/10/40
PT	Lt.	GOETZE Karl	TFD 24/04/42
RO	Uffz.	SEUFERT Rudolf	TFD 24/04/42
PT	Lt.	LEICKHARDT Hans	TFD 01/10/42
RO	Uffz.	GROSSE Herbert	TFD 01/10/42
PT	Uffz.	STÖBER Rudolf	TFD 01/10/42
RO	Uffz.	FRIEDERICH Hans	TFD 01/10/42
PT	Uffz.	VOELSKOW Peter	WIA 29/07/42
RO	Uffz.	SCHWARZ Kurt	KIA 29/07/42
PT	Oblt.	ZOBEL Ernst	WIA 16/10/40
RO	Uffz.	PELLNAT Robert	WIA 16/10/40

3 Staffel

PT	Lt.	ALTENDORF Rudolf	TFD 01/10/42
RO	Uffz.	ARNDT Wilfried	TFD 01/10/42
PT	Lt.	HESSEL Ernst	TFD 18/11/40
RO	Uffz.	HEIDRICH Erich	TFD 18/11/40
PT	Fw.	WARRELMANN Alfred	WIA 07/09/41
RO	Uffz.	(BIEG Hans)	WIA 07/09/41

V/(Z) LG 1

13 Staffel

PT	Lt.	BECK Günter	KIA 13/08/40
PT	Fw.	BRUNS Adolf	KIA 17/09/40
PT	Lt.	BEYER Franz	TFD 01/04/40
RO	Uffz.	BUSCH Paul	WIA 08/08/40
RO	Gefr.	CONRAD Georg	KIA 12/05/40
PT	Fw.	DATZ Hans	POW 13/08/40
RO	Uffz.	DIECKMANN Alfred	WIA 08/08/40
RO	Uffz.	DIERKES Alois	WIA 12/05/40

PT	Lt.	GAFFAL Hans	WIA 12/05/40
RO	Uffz.	GERIGK Walter	KIA 15/09/40
PT	Oblt.	GLIENKE Joachim	KIA 25/08/40
PT	Lt.	GOETZE Karl	KIA 11/01/44
PT	Lt.	GORISCH Ernst	KIA 15/09/40
RO	Gefr.	GRÖBL Franz	KIA 27/09/40
PT	Uffz.	HARTENSTEIN Kurt	KIA 12/05/40
RO	Fw.	HOFFMANN Andreas	KIA 15/09/40
RO	Uffz.	HOYER Karl	KIA 13/08/40
PT	Fw.	JENTZSCH Gerhard	KIA 08/06/40
PT	Fw.	KINZLER Klaus	KIA 04/01/40
PT	Obfw.	KOBERT Rudolf	POW 01/09/40
RO	Uffz.	KOHRT Fritz	DCD 00/00/45
PT	Fw.	KLEVER Georg	WIA 13/08/40
RO	Uffz.	LÄMMEL Georg	KIA 13,08/40
RO	Uffz.	LISCHNEWSKI Bruno	WIA 16/12/43
RO	Fw.	MEINIG Werner	POW 01/09/40
RO	Obgefr.	MÖLLER Paul	KIA 04/01/40
RO	Uffz.	LANDROCK Willi	KIA 04/01/40
PT	Oblt.	MÜLLER Helmut (Kap.)	KIA 15/09/40
RO	Uffz.	PAPE Heino	TFD 18/03/40
RO	Uffz.	PETRY Willi	KIA 26/03/40
PT	Hptm.	PETERS Hellmut (Kap.)	DCD 00/00/45
PT	Lt.	SCHMIDT Ernst	KIA 29/03/40
PT	Lt.	SCHMIDT Hans	DCD 00/00/45
PT	Fw.	SCHOB Herbert	TFD 18/03/40
PT	Lt.	SCHULTZE Helmut	WIA 12/05/40
RO	Uffz.	SCHÜTTE Albert	DCD 00/00/45
RO	Uffz.	SEUFERT Rudolf	DCD 00/00/45
RO	Uffz.	SOLLUCH Georg	KIA 21/05/40
PT	Obfw.	STEGEMANN Alois	KIA 21/05/40
RO	Uffz.	STUCK Paul	KIA 25/08/40
PT	Uffz.	SWIETLIK Paul	KIA 27/09/40
RO	Uffz.	WENIGER Max	KIA 23/03/40
RO	Gefr.	WELZ Heinz	KIA 27/09/40
RO	Uffz.	WIEBE Gustav	DCD 00/00/45
RO	Uffz.	WELLER Hugo	WIA 13/08/40

01/01/1940 to 30/09/1940: Total 45, of which 3 were transferred, 3 POW, 8 wounded, 24 killed; 83% casualties.

14 Staffel

PT	Lt.	ADAMETZ Hugo	KIA 15/09/40
PT	Hptm.	BOLTENSTERN v. Hans (Kap.)	TFD 26/08/40
PT	Uffz.	BECHTHOLD Hans	POW 27/09/40
PT	Lt.	BECKER Ludwig	TFD 01/07/40
PT	Lt.	BRAUKMEIER Hans	KIA 04/09/40
RO	Fw.	BREMSER Karl	KIA 04/09/40
RO	Fw.	BRUNNER Helmut	KIA 08/08/40
PT	Lt.	BONIN v. Eckart	WIA 22/06/43
RO	Obgefr.	DÖPFER Karl	POW 31/06/40
PT	Lt.	EICHHORN Karl	POW 31/08/40
RO	Uffz.	FABIAN Willi	KIA 11/05/40
PT	Oblt.	FENSKE Walter	TFD 21/07/40
RO	Uffz.	FRIEDERICH Hans	DCD 00/00/45
PT	Fw.	FRITZ Gottlob	POW 31/08/40
RO	Obgefr.	GROSSE Herbert	WIA 25/08/40
RO	Uffz.	GROWE Richard	KIA 31/08/40
RO	Gefr.	HAAS Alfred	WIA 13/08/40
RO	Uffz.	HARDER Wilhelm	KIA 21/07/40
RO	Obgefr.	HÜBNER Artur	KIA 27/09/40
RO	Uffz.	JÄCKEL Joachim	POW 04/09/40
PT	Fw.	JECKE Gerhard	WIA 15/08/40
RO	Uffz.	JOHRDEN Friedrich	WIA 22/06/43
PT	Oblt.	JUNGE Michel (Kap.)	KIA 04/09/40
RO	Uffz.	KOCH Hans	KIA 27/09/40
PT	Lt.	KREBITZ Kurt	WIA 13/07/40
RO	Obgefr.	KRISCHEWSKI Josef	KIA 14/09/40
RO	Gefr.	KLEMM Fritz	KIA 13/08/40

PT	Lt.	LEICKHARDT Hans	WIA 11/05/40
PT	Fw.	LINDEMANN Friedrich	KIA 27/09/40
PT	Hptm.	MAUKE Alexander (Kap)	SICK 08/08/40
PT	Oblt.	METHFESSEL Werner (Kap)	KIA 17/05/40
RO	Uffz.	MEINHARD Helmut	DCD 00/00/45
PT	Uffz.	NISIEWICZ Hans	TFD 15/09/40
RO	Uffz.	RADECK Kurt	KIA 29/03/40
RO	Uffz.	RESENER Heinz	KIA 17/05/40
PT	Fw.	RÖHRING Karl	KIA 04/09/40
PT	Lt.	SCHALKHAUSSER Kurt	WIA 17/05/40
RO	Obgefr.	SCHMERGAL Karl	WIA 15/08/40
RO	Obgefr.	SCHMIDT Heinz	KIA 17/05/40
PT	Uffz.	SCHMITT Friedrich	KIA 17/05/40
RO	Fw.	SCHNEIDER Fritz	TFD 26/08/40
RO	Uffz.	SCHWARZ Kurt	KIA 29/07/42
RO	Uffz.	STEINER Alfred	TFD 21/07/40
PT	Uffz.	STÖBER Rudolf.	DCD 00/00/45
RO	Obgefr	STIEF Rudolf	KIA 15/09/40
PT	Fw.	STURM Alfred	KIA 08/08/40
PT	Uffz.	VOELSKOW Peter	WIA 29/07/42
PT	Lt.	WERNER Horst	KIA 13/08/40
PT	Fw.	WÜRGATSCH Horst	KIA 21/07/40

01/01/1940 to 30/09/1940: Total 49, of which 7 were transferred, 5 POW, 8 wounded and 23 killed; 85% casualties.

15 Staffel

RO	Uffz.	ARNDT Heinz	KIA 02/04/40
RO	Uffz.	ARNDT Wilfried	WIA 17/08/43
PT	Lt.	ALTENDORF Rudolf	DCD 00/00/45
RO	Uffz.	BANSER Wilhelm	WIA 04/09/40
RO	Uffz.	BRÜGGOW Horst	POW 27/09/40
RO	Uffz.	BUGRAM Gerhard	TFD 30/08/40
PT	Lt.	BUSCHING Hans	KIA 02/04/40
PT	Olt.	CLAUSEN Walter (Kap.)	KIA 22/04/40
RO	Uffz.	DANNERT Johann	TFD 30/05/40
PT	Lt.	EISELE Hermann	KIA 13/07/40
RO	Gefr.	FRESSEL Walter	TFD 18/08/40
RO	Obgefr.	GIGLHUBER Otto	POW 13/08/40
PT	Oblt.	GRAVENREUTH v. Ulrich (Kap.)	KIA 27/09/40
PT	Uffz.	GROTEN Josef	TFD 20/03/40
PT	Uffz.	HAMANN Horst	KIA 25/08/40
RO	Uffz.	HEIDRICH Erich	TFD 18/11/40
PT	Lt.	HESSEL Ernst	TFD 16/11/40
RO	Uffz.	HELDT Paul	KIA 13/08/40
PT	Fw.	JÄCKEL Martin	KIA 01/09/40
RO	Uffz.	KRAMP Otto	KIA 09/09/40
RO	Uffz.	LOCHOW Kurt	KIA 13/07/40
RO	Uffz.	MARESCH Wenzel	KIA 25/08/40
PT	Uffz.	NEUMANN Wilhelm	KIA 04/09/40
RO	Obgefr.	PETRICH Fritz	KIA 16/05/40
PT	Uffz.	PFAFFELHUBER Alois	KIA 09/09/40
RO	Fw.	REINHOLD Otto	KIA 27/09/40
PT	Lt.	RISSMANN Robert	TFD 01/04/40
RO	Flg.	RÖSLER Heinz	KIA 01/09/40
PT	Oblt.	SCHNOOR Emil (Kap.)	TFD 07/06/40
PT	Uffz.	SCHÜMICHEN Werner	POW 13/06/40
PT	Lt.	SCHWARZER Georg	KIA 16/05/40
RO	Uffz.	SPEIER Walter	KIA 04/09/40
RO	Uffz.	STIER Alfred	TFD 18/08/40
PT	Obfw.	WAGNER Heinz	KIA 13/06/40
PT	Fw.	WARRELMANN Alfred	WIA 11/08/40
PT	Oblt.	WECKEISER Otto	POW 27/09/40

01/01/1940 to 30/09/1940: Total 36, of which 7 were transferred, 4 POW, 2 wounded, 19 killed; 86% casualties.

Documents

Der   U n t e r o f f i z i e r
(Dienstgrad)

der   3. / Nachtjagdgeschwader 3

H o r s t   B r ü g g o w
(Vor- und Zuname)

ist mit Wirkung vom   1. M ä r z   1943   zum

F e l d w e b e l

befördert worden.

, den   1. M ä r z   19 43
(Ort)   (Tag)

I./Nachtjagdgeschwader 3
(Dienststelle)

(Name)

Hauptmann u. Gruppenkommandeur
m. d. W. d. G. b.
(Dienstgrad und Dienststellung)

Bestallung

für den Feldwebel Horst B r ü g g o w
(Dienstgrad, Vor- und Zuname)

der 3./Nachtjagdgeschwader 3

4638   Laporte & Dosse, Amsterdam-W., Sloterdijk

Im Namen des Führers und Obersten Befehlshabers der Wehrmacht

verleihe ich

dem

Unteroffizier

Horst B r ü g g o w

V./(Z.) L.G.1

das

Eiserne Kreuz 1. Klasse.

Stabsquartier ....., den 5. September 19 40 ....

Der Chef der Luftflotte 2
und Befehlshaber Nordwest

Generalfeldmarschall.
(Dienstgrad und Dienststellung)

Im Namen des Führers und Obersten Befehlshabers der Wehrmacht

verleihe ich

dem

Gefreiten B r ü g g o w

von der V.(Z)/L.G.1

das

Eiserne Kreuz 2. Klasse.

B e r l i n , den 29. Sept. 1939.

Generalmajor u. Kdr. d. Ltw. Lehr-Div.
(Dienstgrad und Dienststellung)

Im Namen des führers
und Oberften Befehlshabers
der Wehrmacht

verleihe ich

dem

Obergefreiten Willfried Arndt

das

Eiferne Kreuz 2.Klaffe.

Im Felde.........,den ..31.Juli.......1940..

Der Kommandierende General
des VIII.Fliegerkorps

General der Flieger
(Dienftgrad und Dienftftellung)

Im Namen des führers
und Oberften Befehlshabers
der Wehrmacht

verleihe ich

dem

Unteroffizier
Willfried Arndt
I./N.J.G.3

das

Eiferne Kreuz 1.Klaffe.

Stabsquartier....,den...13...Januar.19..41

Der Chef der Luftflotte 2
und Befehlshaber Nordwest

Generalfeldmarschall
(Dienftgrad und Dienftftellung)

Verleihungsurkunde

Im Namen des
Oberbefehlshabers der Luftwaffe

verleihe ich dem

Unteroffizier Willfried **A r n d t**

der 3./N.J.G. 3

die

Frontflug=Spange für Jäger
in Silber

im Felde , den 1. Juli 194 1

Major und Geschwaderkommodore.

Verleihungsurkunde

Im Namen des
Oberbefehlshabers der Luftwaffe

verleihe ich dem

Feldwebel Wilfried **A r n d t**

2./ Nachtjagdgeschwader 4

die

Frontflug=Spange für Nacht=Jäger
in Gold

Gefechtsstand, den 7.Juni 1943

Oberst und Geschwaderkommodore.

Im Namen des Führers
und Obersten Befehlshabers
der Wehrmacht

verleihe ich

dem

Gefreiten S c h m e r g a l

von der V.(Z)/L.G.1

das

Eiserne Kreuz 2.Klasse.

B e r l i n , den 29. Sept. 1939.

Generalmajor u. Kdr. d. Lw.-Lehr-Div.

(Dienstgrad und Dienststellung)

Im Namen des Führers
und Obersten Befehlshabers
der Wehrmacht

verleihe ich

dem

Gefreiter Karl S c h m e r g a l
14./(Zerstörer)Lehrgeschwader 1

das

Eiserne Kreuz 1.Klasse.

Lfl..H..Qu..., den 29. August 1940.

Generalfeldmarschall
Chef der Luftflotte 3
und Befehlshaber West

(Dienstgrad und Dienststellung)

Der   Unteroffizier
(Dienstgrad)

de r   2. / Nachtjagdgeschwader 3
(Truppenteil usw.)

Karl   S c h m e r g a l
(Vor- und Familienname)

ist mit Wirkung vom   1. September 1942   zum

F e l d w e b e l

befördert worden.

Gefechtsstand   , den 1. September 194 2
(Ort)   (Tag)

I./ Nachtjagdgeschwader 3
(Dienststelle)

(Name)

Hauptmann u. Gruppenkommandeur

M. d. W. d. G. b.
(Dienstgrad und Dienststellung)

Bestallung

für den   Feldwebel
(Dienstgrad)

Karl S c h m e r g a l
(Vor- und Familienname)

de r   2./ Nachtjagdgeschwader 3
(Truppenteil usw.)

60. **Luftw.** 8. 41. Kroll & Straus, Berlin SO. 36 — Din A 4

Verleihungsurkunde

Im Namen des
Oberbefehlshabers der Luftwaffe

verleihe ich dem

Unteroffizier Karl Schmergal

(Bordfunker)

die

Frontflug-Spange für Jäger

in Silber

Stabsquartier , den 19.März 1941
Der Kommandierende General
des X. Fliegerkorps

General der Flieger

Verleihungsurkunde

Im Namen des
Oberbefehlshabers der Luftwaffe

verleihe ich dem

Unteroffizier Karl Schmergal

die

Frontflug-Spange für Jäger

in Gold

Stabsquartier , den 3.Juli 1941
Der Kommandierende General
des X. Fliegerkorps

General der Flieger

Im Namen des Führers und Obersten Befehlshabers der Wehrmacht

verleihe ich

dem

Unteroffizier Albert K ö p g e
Stab/(Z) L.G. 1

das

Eiserne Kreuz 2. Klasse.

Gefechtsstand, den 15. Juli 1940
Der Kommandierende General
des IV. Flieger - Korps

General der Flieger
(Dienstgrad und Dienststellung)

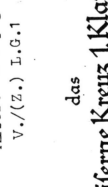

Im Namen des Führers und Obersten Befehlshabers der Wehrmacht

verleihe ich

dem

Unteroffizier
Albert K ö p g e
V./(Z.) L.G.1

das

Eiserne Kreuz 1. Klasse.

Stabsquartier, den 5. September 19.40
Der Chef der Luftflotte 2
und Befehlshaber Nordwest

Generalfeldmarschall.
(Dienstgrad und Dienststellung)

Luftwaffenbordfunkerschein

Land

Nr. 11

für Unteroffizier Albert Köpge
(Dienstgrad, Vor- und Zuname)

geboren: 8. 1. 1916

Diensteintritt: 1.10.35
Truppenteil: 4./Fea 47 Stade

Inhaber ist befördert

zum . . . am . . .
zum . . . am . . .
zum . . . am . . .
zum . . . am . . .

Stab/K. G. 53
(Ausstellende Dienststelle)

Ansbach, den 17. Okt. 1939
(Ort)   (Datum)

Albert Köpge
(Eigenh. Unterschrift, Bord-U. Zuname)

Am 27.9.1940 starb der
Unteroffizier
Albert Köpge

den Heldentod für Führer,
Volk und Vaterland.

Im Auftrage des Reichsministers der
Luftfahrt und Oberbefehlshabers der
Luftwaffe ist darüber diese Urkunde
ausgestellt worden.

O.U., den 22.9.1941

Hauptmann und Kommandeur

Am 27.9.1940 starb der

Hauptmann
Horst Liensberger

den Heldentod für Führer,
Volk und Vaterland.

Im Auftrage des Reichsministers der
Luftfahrt und Oberbefehlshabers der
Luftwaffe ist darüber diese Urkunde
ausgestellt worden.

W.Qu., den 22.9.1941

Hauptmann und Kommandeur

Im Namen des Führers
und Obersten Befehlshabers
der Wehrmacht

verleihe ich

dem

Hauptmann Horst Liensberger
Kommandeur
v.(Z)/Lehrgeschwader 1

das

Eiserne Kreuz 1.Klasse.

Lfl. Hpt. Qu., den 22. Mai 19.40.

General der Flieger
Chef der Luftflotte 3
u.Befehlshaber West
(Dienstgrad und Dienststellung)

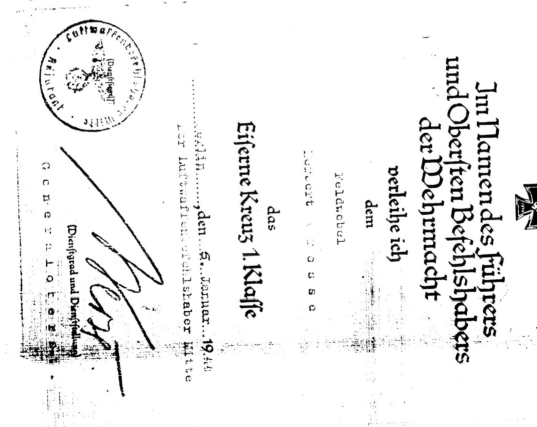

Ich verleihe
dem

Hauptmann

Horst Liensberger

in Anerkennung seiner vorbildlichen Tapferkeit

und der erfolgreichen Führung seiner Gruppe

den Ehrenpokal
für besondere Leistung
im Luftkrieg

Hauptquartier des Ob. d. L., den 28.August 1940

Der Reichsminister der Luftfahrt
und Oberbefehlshaber der Luftwaffe,

Reichsmarschall

Jm Namen
des
führers und Reichskanzlers
befördere ich

den Oberleutnant in der Luftwaffe

Horst Liensberger

mit Wirkung vom 1. Juni 1938 zum

Hauptmann

Ich vollziehe diese Urkunde in der Erwartung,
daß der Genannte getreu seinem Diensteide
seine Berufspflichten gewissenhaft erfüllt und
das Vertrauen rechtfertigt, das ihm durch
diese Beförderung bewiesen wird. Zugleich
darf er des besonderen Schutzes des führers
und Reichskanzlers sicher sein.

Berlin, den   23. Mai 1938

Der Reichsminister der Luftfahrt
und Oberbefehlshaber der Luftwaffe

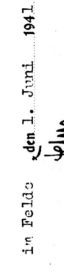

Verleihungsurkunde

Im Namen des
Oberbefehlshabers der Luftwaffe

verleihe ich dem

Unteroffizier Hellmut M e i n h a r d

der 2./N.J.G. 3

die

Frontflug-Spange für Jäger

in Bronze

im Felde, den 1. Juni 1941

[signature]

Major und Geschwaderkommodore.

Im Namen des Führers und Obersten Befehlshabers der Wehrmacht

verleihe ich

dem

Unteroffizier Helmut M e i n h a r d
14./ (Z) L.G. 1

das

Eiserne Kreuz 2. Klasse.

Gefechtsstand, den 15. Juli 1940.

Der Kommandierende General
des IV. Flieger - Korps

[signature] Pflugbeil

General der Flieger,
(Dienstgrad und Dienststellung)

Der   Unteroffizier
(Dienstgrad)

der   I./ Nachtjagdgeschwader 4, 2. Staffel
(Truppenteil usw.)

Hans -Hartmut B e c h t h o l d
(Vor- und Familienname)

ist mit Wirkung vom   1. Juni 1943   zum

Feldwebel

befördert worden.

Gefechtsstand   , den 1. Juni   194
(Ort)   (Tag)

I./Nachtjagdgeschwader 4
(Dienststelle)

(Name)

(Dienstgrad und Dienststelle)
Hauptmann u. Gruppenkommandeur
m.d.W.d.G.b.

Bestallung

für den   Feldwebel
(Dienstgrad)

Hans- Hartmut Bechthold
(Vor- und Familienname)

de   2./N.J.G. 4
(Truppenteil usw.)

Wurde mir in die
Gefangenschaft zugeschickt! —

— obwohl ich kein Nachtjäger war!

60. Luftw. 8. 41. Kroll & Straus, Berlin SO. 36 — Din A 4

Verleihungsurkunde

Ich verleihe dem

Unteroffizier Hans Bechtold

das Abzeichen für

Flugzeugführer

Berlin, den 8. Juli 1939

Der Reichsminister der Luftfahrt
und Oberbefehlshaber der Luftwaffe

I.A.

Kastner

Generalmajor

Nr. 18632 / 39

Index

NOTES

NOTES

NOTES

NOTES

NOTES

NOTES

NOTES

HAUPTMANN J. LIENSBERGER
GERMAN AIR FORCE

27.9.40

THE BRITISH RED CROSS SOCIETY
AND
ORDER OF ST. JOHN

is forwarding a Photograph of the Grave of

Name _Liensberger_

Rank and Initials _Hauptmann J_

Regiment _German Air Force_

Position of Grave _Hailsham Cemetery_

All communications respecting this Photograph should quote the
number ....._787_.....and be addressed to:—

THE BRITISH RED CROSS SOCIETY
AND
ORDER OF ST. JOHN
7 BELGRAVE SQUARE
LONDON, S.W.